WHERE DOES THE PARALLEL WORLD EXIST?

MARI ISHIKAWA

Jewellery & Photography

With essays by
Monika Fahn, Otto Künzli, Jorunn Veiteberg and Gabriella Zaharias-Doff

arnoldsche ART PUBLISHERS

L–R from left to right
T–B from top to bottom

CONTENTS

Parallel with Nature.
The Beauty of Jewellery

MONIKA FAHN

What is reality? What is beauty? These are questions posed by Mari Ishikawa. Born and raised in Japan, she spent the initial years of her career working as an interior decorator and a designer. Seeking an artistic profession in which she could perform all of the steps in the process herself, Mari Ishikawa arrived at jewellery, an activity which occupies a unique position in many respects. Jewellery evades classification as an art, an applied art or a craft. So what is jewellery? Jewellery fascinates, jewellery beautifies, jewellery attracts, jewellery stands out, jewellery touches, jewellery expresses feelings, jewellery is evocative, jewellery vexes, jewellery catches the eye, jewellery adorns. Jewellery makes an impact, and it does so on many different levels. Since the earliest days of human history, people have worn jewellery: the oldest known jewellery finds are now believed to date from over 70,000 years ago.

Why do we wear jewellery? Jewellery is not just a status symbol or beautiful accessory – its impact extends far beyond its aesthetic function. Since time immemorial, jewellery has been the mark of social rank and the expression of a role: think of kings and church dignitaries. Jewellery also illustrates the wealth of its wearer. The Vikings, for example, wore neck rings of gold and silver of more than a kilo in weight. Jewellery is an expression of personality. As soon as our ancestors developed a sense of self-awareness they began distinguishing themselves from nature – comprising animals, plants and natural forces – but also from other members of human society. Jewellery possesses a magical effect. Even our ancestors decorated themselves with animal teeth, claws, feathers and other symbols of strength and beauty. Wearing a charm or talisman was meant to bring luck or protect against evil. An archetypal item of jewellery is the ring, an early currency and a symbol of the bond between two people, with the engagement ring and wedding ring dating back to early Christian times. It is also said that jewellery carries a little of the soul of the person who wore it: think of grandmother's ring, or mourning jewellery. To this day, people feel the need to express their style, their individuality and their values through jewellery. They do so with extremely valuable materials like gold and silver, alongside precious stones. Jewellery is not unambiguous and today, more than ever, appears to occupy and to mark interfaces and ambivalences. Jewellery is a type of non-verbal communication with our fellow man. It can be a social statement.

In Europe we have a long tradition of jewellery design; in Japan the situation is quite the opposite. Traditional Japanese clothing dispenses with most jewellery, the country having only opened up to Western influences from 1868 onwards. So what is it that inspires Mari Ishikawa? Which influences have an effect on her jewellery? It is nature that fascinates her and captures her imagination. The beauty of nature is simply destined to be realised in imagination and in art. Just think of the words of Johann Wolfgang von Goethe: 'Nature! We are surrounded by her and locked in her clasp: powerless to leave her, and powerless to come closer to her. Unasked and unwarned she takes us up into the whirl of her dance and hurries on with us till we are weary and fall from her arms.'[1] Nature is an artful creator on the one hand and an infinite source of inspiration for art on the other. 'Anyone to whom nature begins to unveil its open mystery feels an irresistible yearning for nature's noblest interpreter, for art,' as Goethe put it.[2]

What matters is whether and to what extent the artist reproduces nature or takes it as the starting point for a composition and a creation in its own right. Leon Battista Alberti (1404–1472) already denigrated the reproduction of nature in his works on art theory, postulating that the artist should not 'merely make all parts similar' but should 'also bestow a beauty'.[3] Even at the point of origin, nature is designed to be transient. Art succeeds in capturing moments of being, conserving them for all time. 'Nature is always the same, but nothing about her that we see lasts. Our art must convey a glimmer of her endurance with the elements, the appearance of all her changes. It must give us the sense of her eternity. [...] An artist is only a receptacle for sensations, a brain, a recording device. [...] Art is a harmony parallel with nature,'[4] wrote Paul Cézanne (1839–1906).

Mari Ishikawa involves herself fully with her surroundings and is mindfully observant. She experiences nature with all her senses; she is wholly open to the smallest details, discerning and interpreting the aesthetic of things. Since moving to Germany in 1994, she has had even more direct access to nature. Her notion is that we are moving in a parallel world which constantly surrounds us but which no one notices in the daily grind. Mari Ishikawa asks, 'Where does a parallel world exist? In a different universe? Can one discover such a world through time travel? Is it perhaps possible to see such a world in a dream? Or does it only exist in one's heart? The world we see is only a part of the entire reality which is composed of many worlds existing simultaneously, side by side. We can find a parallel world whenever we open our eyes and hearts. It is always with us.'[5] But only when we sharpen our own gaze do we perceive the beauties by the wayside. And some things require different times of day in order to be discerned. Mari Ishikawa seeks out places in different lighting conditions and captures the natural details in photographs. She is particularly fascinated by moonlight, which makes things appear completely differently. Photography reaches a further dimension of the visible. Long exposures reveal what the human eye cannot see, and we ask ourselves: Is this the parallel world?

In the Western world we focus on the visible. The architect Louis I. Kahn (1901–1974) speaks of light as the creator of all things.[6] In light, forms, textures and colours appear clear and distinct to us. The Japanese aesthetic, on the other hand, places considerable emphasis on shadows. 'A phosphorescent jewel gives off its glow and colour in the dark and loses its beauty in the light of day. Were it not for shadows, there would be no beauty,'[7] wrote Japanese novelist Jun'ichirō Tanizaki (1886–1965). It is exactly the semi-darkness and the disturbing gloom that show off the radiance of certain materials to most impressive effect. The elegance of lacquered surfaces, the glint of the gold and silver thread in old textiles find expression only in the play of shadows between the objects. The colour and structure of Japanese paper needs the twilight in order to be seen to full effect. 'The quality that we call beauty, however, must always grow from the realities of life, and our ancestors, forced to live in dark rooms, presently came to discover beauty in shadows, ultimately to guide shadows towards beauty's end,'[8] explained Jun'ichirō Tanizaki. One of the key words in Japanese aesthetics is *yûgen*. *Yû* expresses a sense of illusion and shadowiness, the immateriality of things. *Gen* describes darkness, dullness or blackness. The beauty of *yûgen* is unfathomable, mysterious and mystical; it rests on the recognition of the immateriality and the limitations of human perception. 'It is beauty borne of spiritual inspiration and yearning motivated by a desire to possess sensory images of the inexpressible, extrasensory reality enveloped in eternal silence and remaining a mystery that lies in the very heart of the phenomenal world.'[9]

We must be observant; we must pause and learn to look. Then we will see the almost lavish beauty that surrounds us. Is it the yellowish shimmer of lichen on a tree trunk or the proudly upward-striving blossoms of a flower? Sometimes, we cannot believe our eyes when we see the details that disclose themselves to the observant eye. Nature challenges us to look diligently, to get to the bottom of things. All of us walk past trees and stones every day of our lives but we seldom perceive their beauty. The potential of beauty begins in its singularity. 'Uniqueness transforms each being into presence, which, in the image of a flower or a tree, never ceases to open, in time, toward the plenitude of its radiance, which is the very definition of beauty,'[10] wrote Chinese novelist, calligrapher and poet François Cheng (born 1929).

What aesthetic does Mari Ishikawa find? She overcomes the transience of nature by collecting natural elements: leaves, blossoms, pieces of bark. Employing the technique of natural casting, she casts the pieces in metal, usually silver. The object being cast is coated in a thin layer of wax and then encased in a plaster mould. The resulting mould is heated, whereupon the wax and the vegetation flow out, leaving behind a mould cavity in the jacket of plaster. The plaster mould sets hard in the fire and then serves as a casting mould. Now the liquid metal, often silver, can be poured in. Once the metal has solidified, the plaster mould is smashed and discarded, which is why the process is also known as lost-mould casting. The cast blank is now ready for fine machining and finishing. Natural casting has been done in this form for centuries. Early examples from the fifteenth century can be found in Padua. Lorenzo Ghiberti (1378–1455) used natural casting to depict trees on his portals at Florence Baptistery. In the first half of the sixteenth century, we begin to see animal casts appearing in the art of the Nuremberg goldsmiths – for example, that of Wenzel Jamnitzer (1507/08–1585) in one of his main works, the *Merkelsche Tafelaufsatz* table ornament from 1549. Natural casting either manifests itself as a work of art in its own right, mostly in a small format – for instance, as a receptacle in the form of an inkwell – or adorns larger vessels like goblets.

Mari Ishikawa uses the silver natural casts as the basis for her jewellery. By applying this technique she manages to render the natural textures of lichens, leaves and blossoms in silver. Then begins the process of artistic creation: passing through many individual steps, the cast becomes a piece of jewellery in its own right with a very specific aesthetic. Mari Ishikawa loves combinations with other materials: diamonds, coral, pearls, but she also chooses traditional Japanese paper. This is where we sense her inner world, her Japanese homeland, whose traditions and aesthetic vocabulary she has maintained though so far away. Pieces of jewellery in various groups are the result, predominantly necklaces, brooches and rings.

The *Moonlight Shadow* and *Parallel Worlds* series are completely dedicated to nature. The visual appearance of the forests, meadows and riverscapes is shaped by the vegetation's rich vocabulary of forms and the intense interplay of greens. This is a very special colour: it can neither be fixed nor can it be used for colouring. As a result, we see green only in nature itself and should make ourselves aware of the distinctiveness of this colour impression. The seasons and the alternating day and night create continual changes in perception. If we look at nature in the moonlight, we see the colours changing, the green transforming into nuanced shades of grey. Here, once again, we come across a parallel world that we can see for a few short hours. Mari Ishikawa realises the grey with natural casts in silver, which she partly blackens to increase the shadowiness and plasticity. Other materials and form elements are also integrated: little strings of beads, extremely fine silver mesh, spiky silver chains. The outcome: sensitive compositions, miniature worlds.

Mari Ishikawa calls another of her groups *Landscape*. The relationship between nature and architecture is central here, both of which exist side by side yet in a state of constant reciprocity. Anything built by the hand of man must be actively preserved otherwise it will be reclaimed by nature. Plant components cast in silver form the basis of the *Landscape* jewellery. The architecture is realised in the form of ground plan elements. Here, Mari Ishikawa uses aluminium curtain rails, carefully prepared. The two elements run through one another, with a link created by red paint, sparingly applied, which envelops the plant world and the architectural world like an organic element.

Memory is the name of another group. Everything is finite and limited; nothing can escape its destiny of one day no longer being there. The engineered world, on the other hand, gives us the impression that storage media can conserve everything for eternity. With this jewellery, Mari Ishikawa's desire is to offer something in response to the finite nature of things, to capture memories. The use of watch parts and storage modules is thus an attempt to fix some things in place – at least visually – for the long term.

In her creative process, Mari Ishikawa herself becomes a creator, making elements grow and proliferate as nature does. In doing so, she develops an aesthetic all of her own. The jewellery of Mari Ishikawa is mysterious and takes us into another world. Her necklaces, brooches and rings are multifaceted and extremely uniform pieces of jewellery which look as if they're naturally grown. In making them, Mari Ishikawa captures an eternal moment that would otherwise be continuously changing. A close look at her jewellery also gives rise to poetic moments and summons stories and memories that cause us to pause. Mari Ishikawa's jewellery is an illustration of the beauty that surrounds us, even in the apparently banal. We should accept the invitation to look more carefully next time we're out for a walk. Then and only then will we become aware of the beauty and the richness of the world in which we live.

1 Johann Wolfgang von Goethe, *Fragment über die Natur, Hamburger Ausgabe*, Hamburg 1981, Vol. 13, p. 45.
2 Johann Wolfgang von Goethe, *Goethes Werke. Vollständige Ausgabe letzter Hand*, Stuttgart/Tübingen 1833, Vol. 49: *Maximen und Reflexionen*, p. 66.
3 Leon Battista Alberti, *Kleinere kunsttheoretische Schriften*, ed. and transl. Hubert Janitschek, 1877, reprint Osnabrück 1970, pp. 150–151.
4 *Conversations with Cézanne*, ed. Michael Doran, Berkeley 2001, p. 9.
5 Gesellschaft für Goldschmiedekunst e.V. and Deutsches Goldschmiedehaus Hanau (eds.), *Mari Ishikawa. Parallel Worlds*, Hanau 2011, p. 21.
6 Romaldo Giurgola and Jaimini Mehta, *Louis I. Kahn*, Zurich 1979, p. 17.
7 Jun'ichirō Tanizaki, *In Praise of Shadows*, transl. Thomas J. Harper and Edward G. Seidensticker, New Haven 1977, p. 53.
8 Ibid., p. 33.
9 Toshihiko Izutsu and Toyo Izutsu, *The Theory of Beauty in the Classical Aesthetics of Japan*, The Hague 1981, p. 44.
10 François Cheng, *The Way of Beauty. Five Meditations for Spiritual Transformation*, Rochester 2009, p. 24.

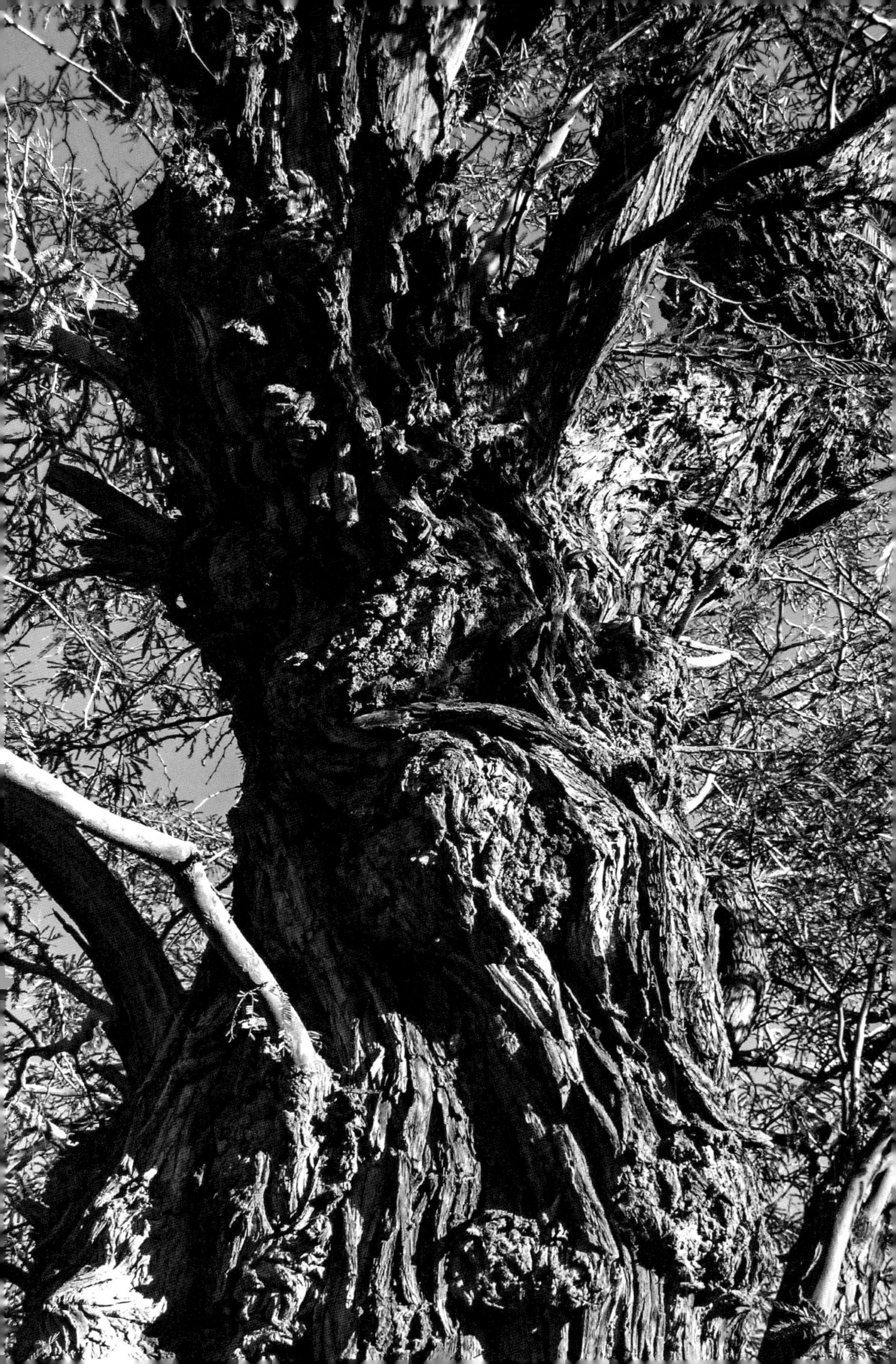

Where does the parallel world exist?

Can one discover this world through

Is it perhaps possible to see this world

Or does it only exist in one's heart?

The world we see is only a part of the

which is composed of many worlds

simultaneously, side by side

We can find "Parallel worlds" whenever

our eyes

They are always with us

Where does the parallel world exist?

Can one discover this world through time travel?
Is it perhaps possible to see this world in a dream?
Or does it only exist in one's heart?

The world we see is only a part of the entire reality,
which is composed of many worlds exsting
simultaneously, side by side

We can find "Parallel worlds" whenever we open
our eyes

They are always with us

LOVE MAKES BLIND

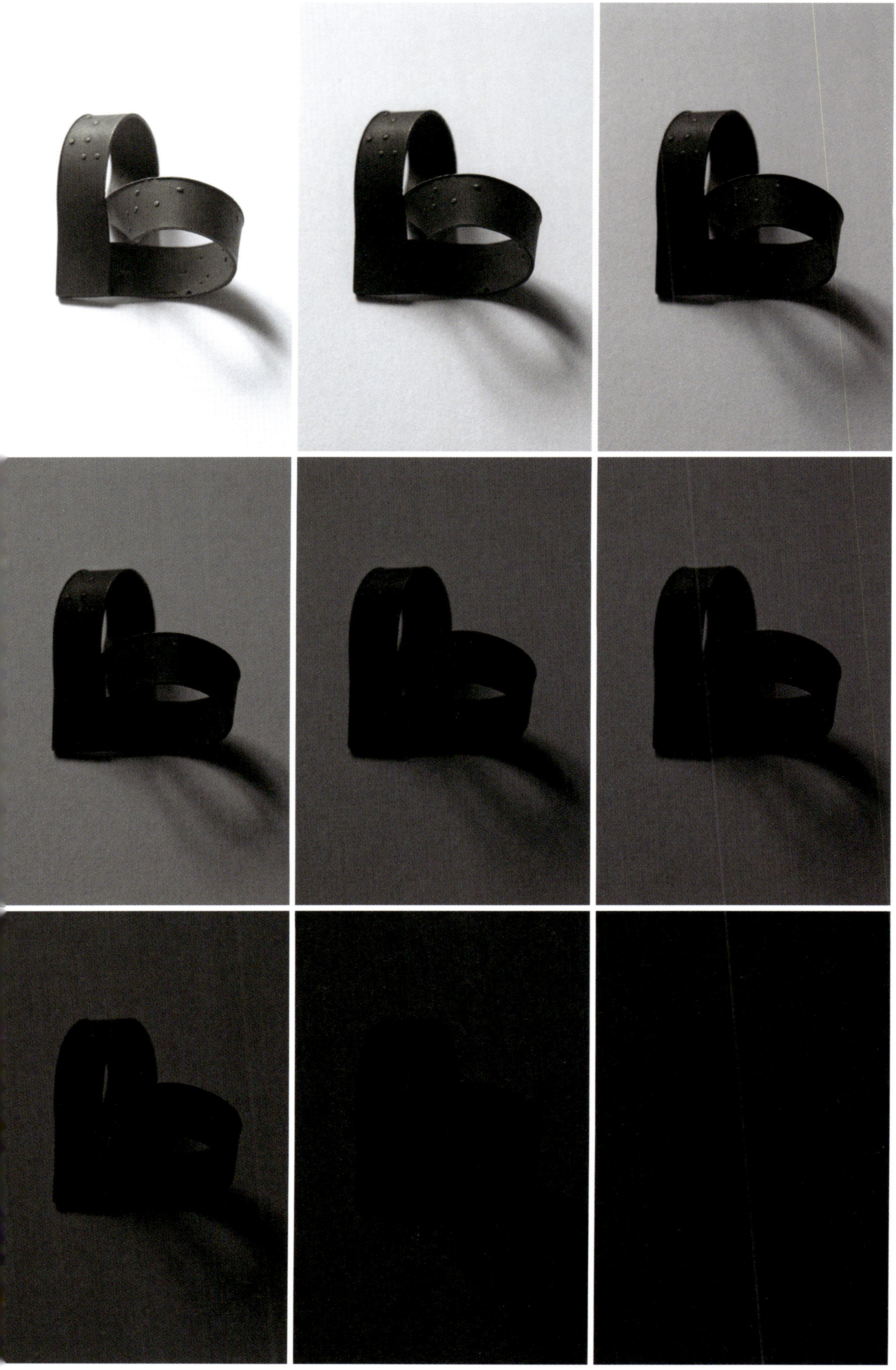

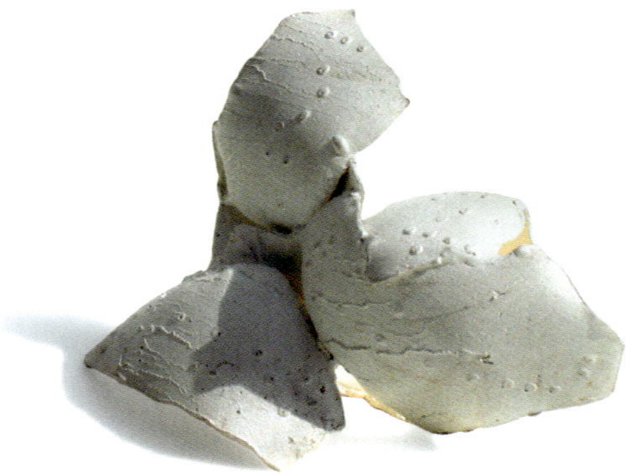

Brooch, 2004, 50 × 40 × 25 mm, 925 silver

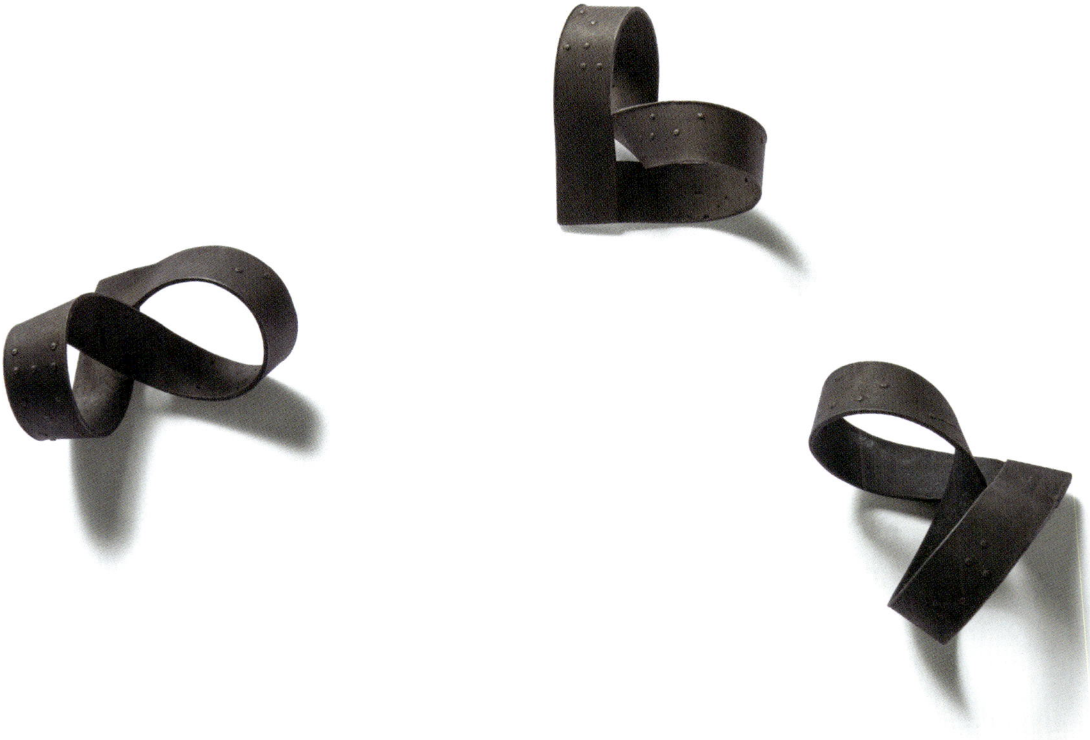

Ring, 1999, 50 × 40 × 25 mm, 925 silver, oxidized

SHADOW

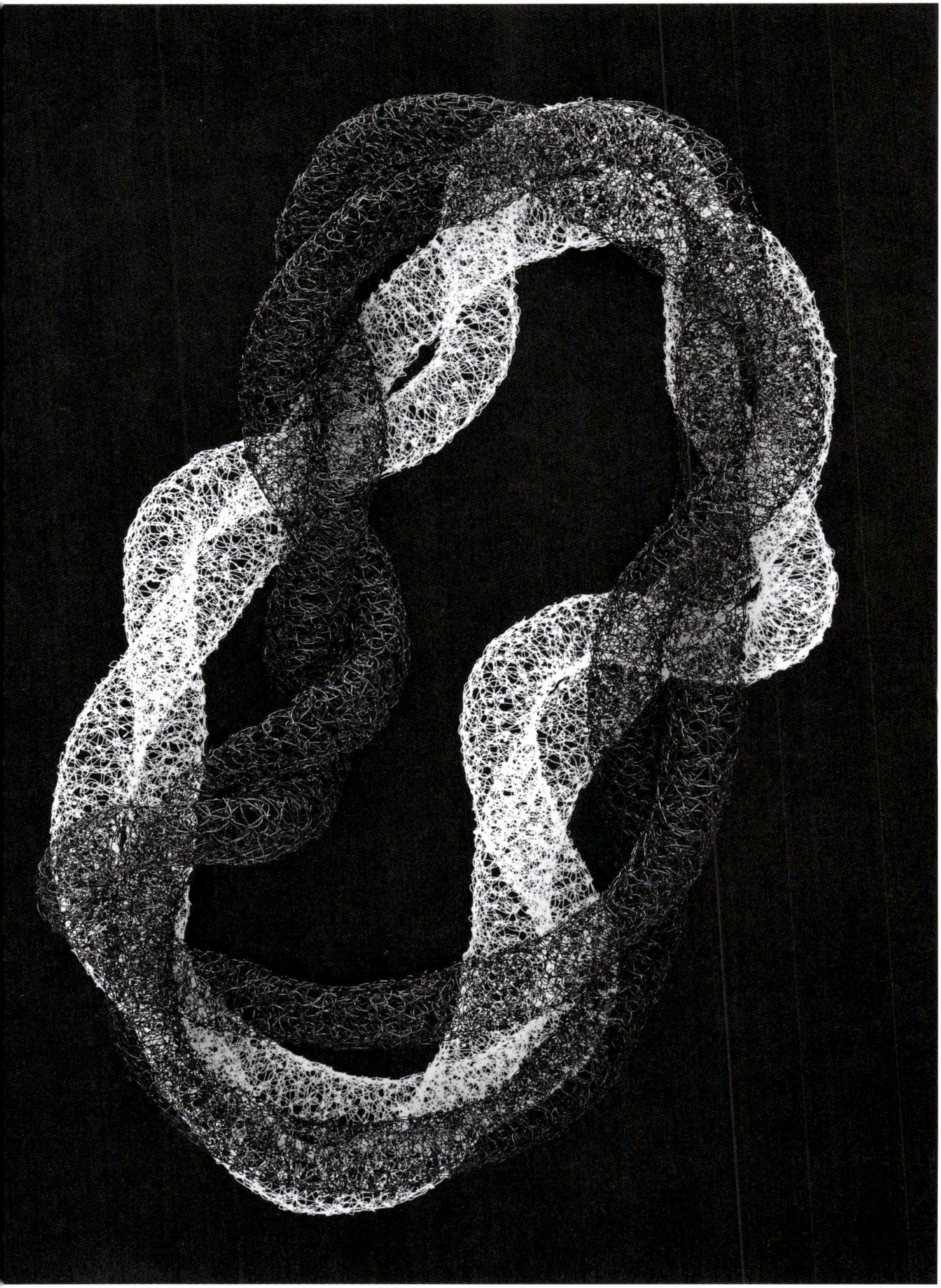

eckpiece, 2000, 800 mm long, steel, glass beads
hotogram, 2000, 450 × 300 × 5 mm, photo paper, aluminium panel

Brooches, 1999, T–B 110 × 65 × 50 mm, 90 × 70 × 55 mm, 105 × 60 × 55 mm, 925 silver, Japanese lacquer
Photograms, 1999, each 235 × 175 × 5 mm, photo paper, aluminium panel

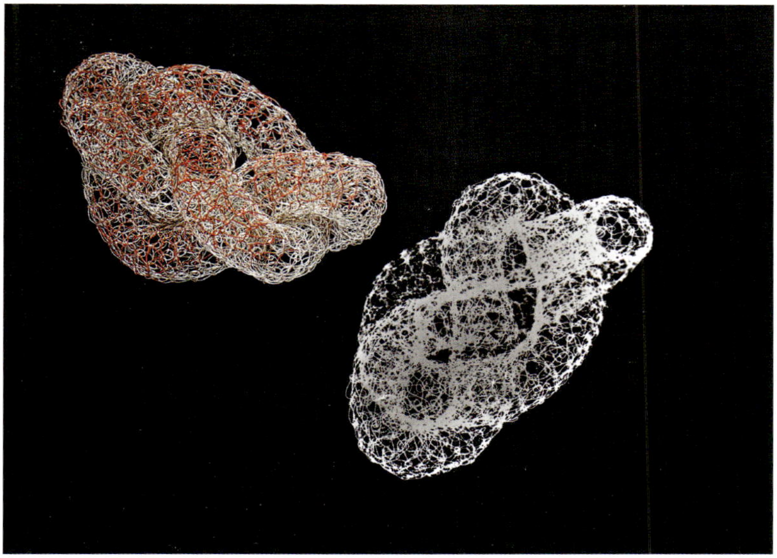

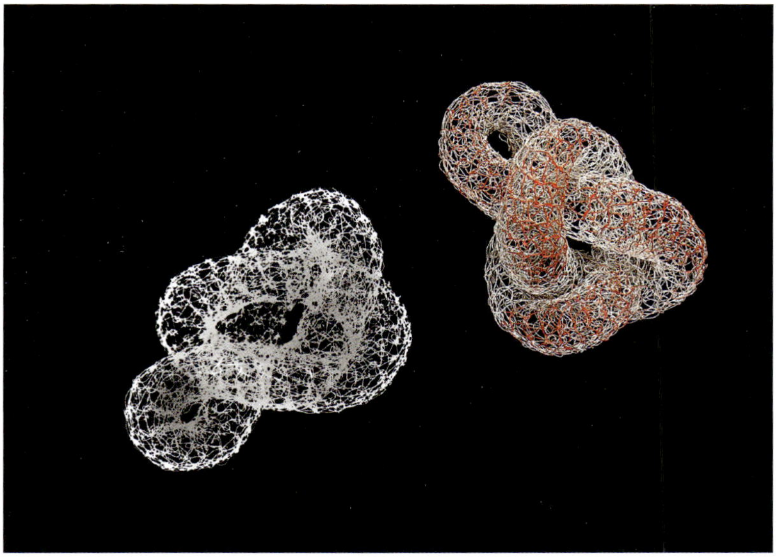

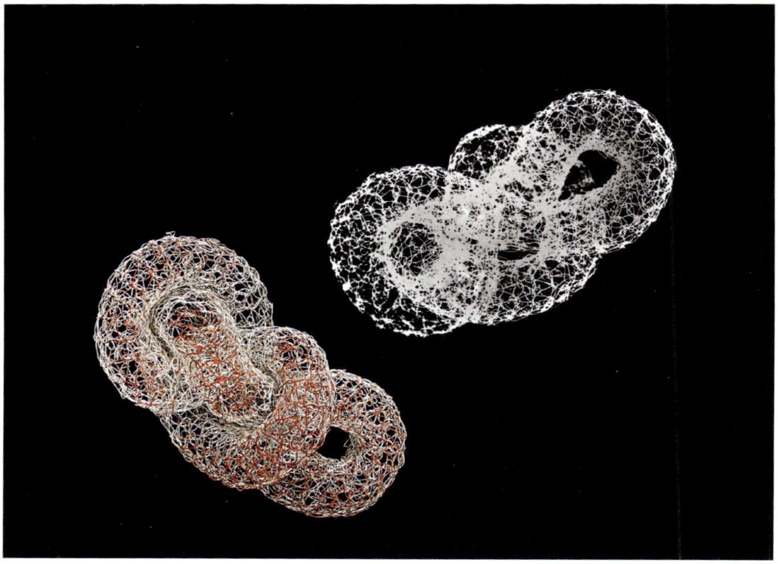

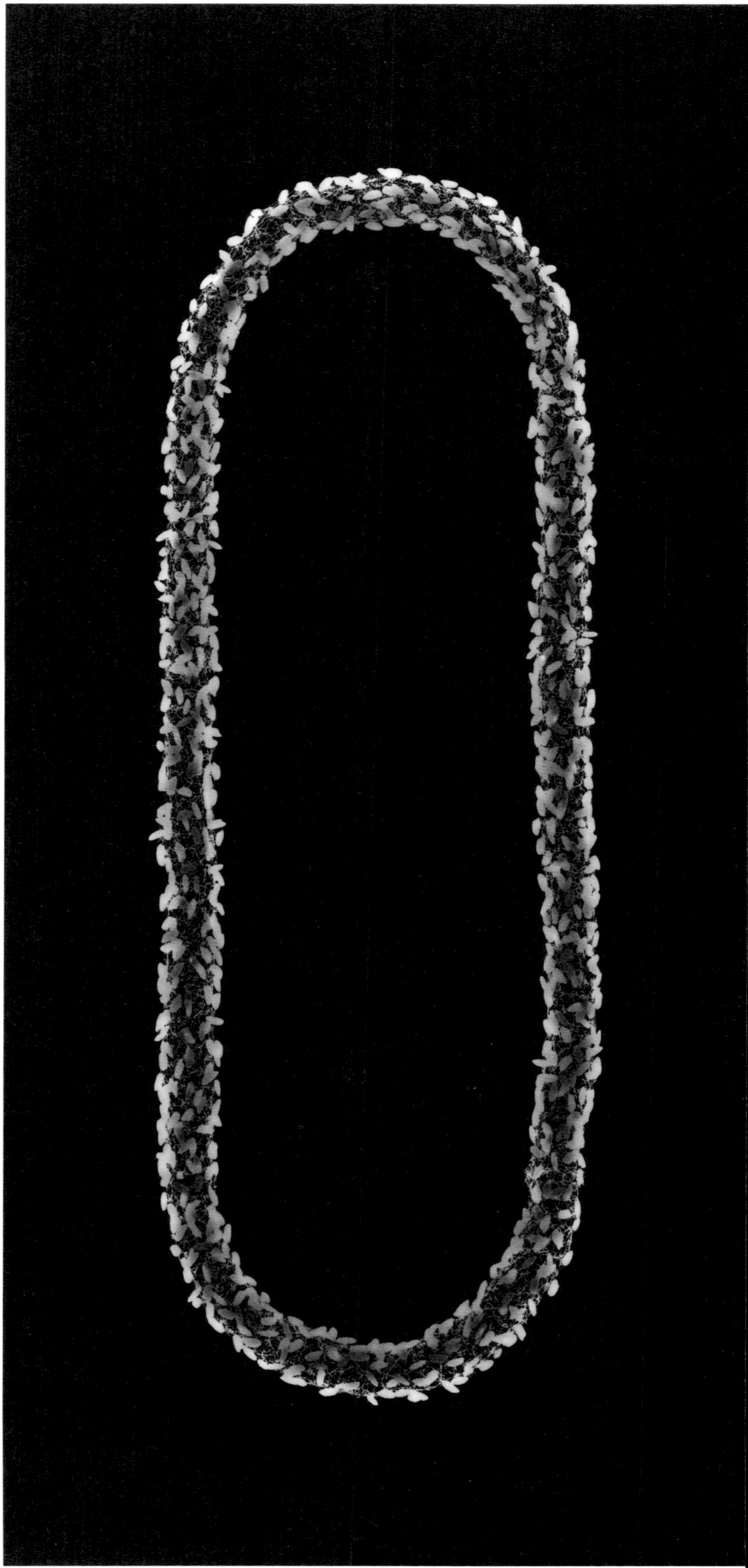

THE LAND
OF THE RISING SUN

Photogram, 2001,
500 × 250 × 5 mm,
photo paper,
aluminium panel

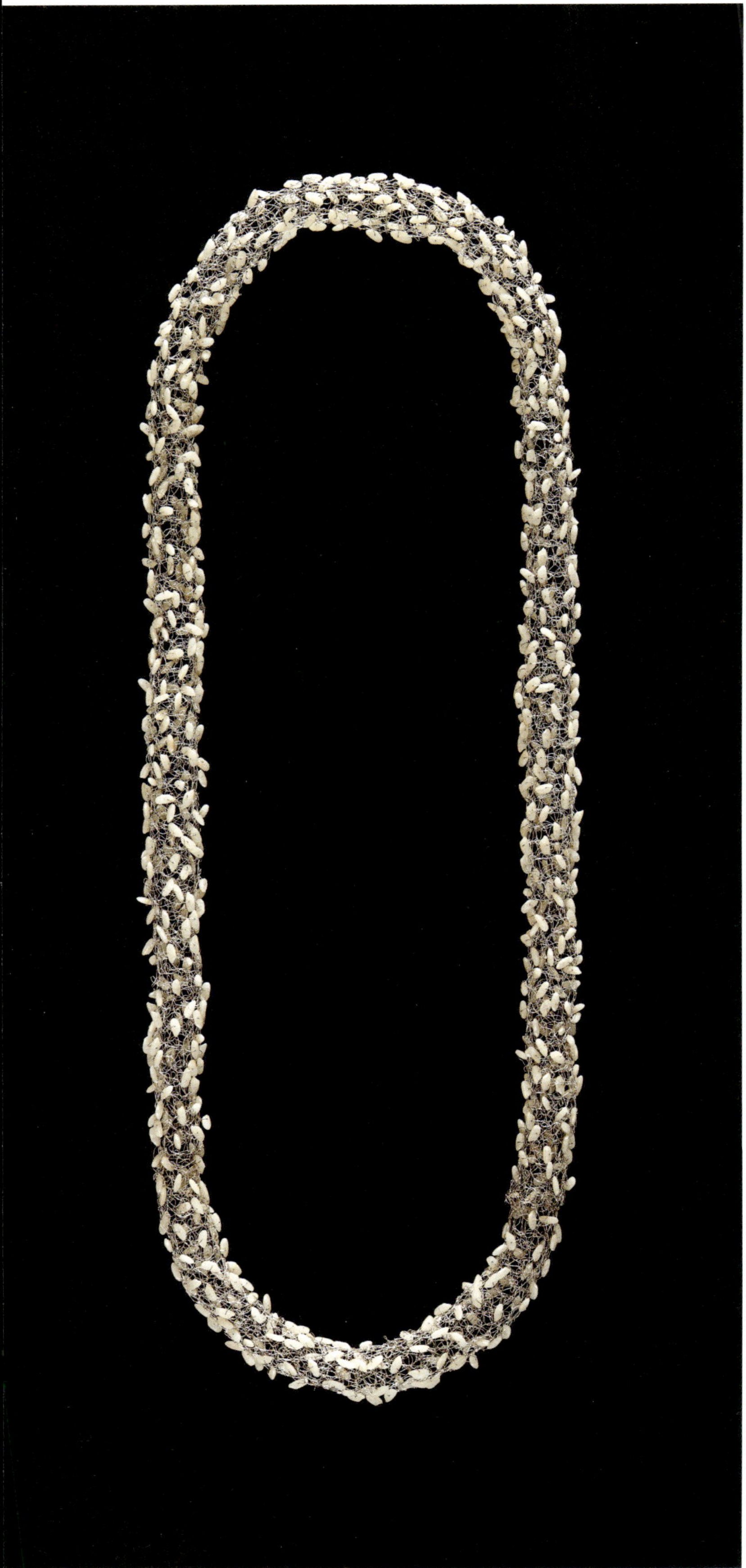

Neckpiece, 2001,
900 mm long,
925 silver, rice

Panel, 500 × 250 × 5 mm,
photo paper,
aluminium panel

Mr White Hagi

OTTO KÜNZLI

'Mari-chan! You mustn't play with your food!'
Thus or similarly, Mari Ishikawa, like most children in Japan, and all over the world, was admonished by her mother to treat food decorously and with respect.

Three decades later, in 2000, Mari Ishikawa made a piece of jewellery from rice. Innumerable grains of rice circle about the wearer's neck, orbiting it like a channelled blizzard, like a 'dust ring' round Saturn.

According to Mari Ishikawa her mother has started worrying again about whether her daughter still plays with her food ...

Time machine. Japan, in the mountains. Where Narayama Ballads[1] were sung:
'Surviving winter is a hard thing to do each year.[2] *My goodness, how clever my father is; he's hardly been ill for three days but he already has his rice.*[3] *Mr White Hagi,*[4] *that's what rice was called. A god lived on Narayama*[5] *and since everyone knew the god was there, a festival was celebrated at which, besides the early fruits of autumn and chestnuts from the forest and wild berries, the fruits of the Shii and the Kaja,*[6] *besides wild mushrooms, rice was also cooked and eaten, the most precious thing in existence ...*[7] *They eat too much at home.'*[8]
But still there wasn't enough for everyone. Granny Oma O Rin knew that as soon as the first snow fell, it was time to set out for Narayama. Weeks before, she had already brutally knocked some of her healthy teeth out of her jaw but was ashamed that she could still chew and eat so well. She left the house at daybreak. It was the rule not to look back.
'How many ravens there are in the mountains.'[9]

For her neckpiece Mari Ishikawa drilled the minutest of holes through each grain and strung them on silver wire as thin as hair, which in turn was woven into a sort of cord that now follows a cosmic track without beginning and end.

Yamato[10] – the marked sense of community that shapes Japanese society, being considerate of each other in the most cramped space imaginable – derives, as I have been told, from growing, sowing, irrigating and harvesting rice, which could only be managed cooperatively. The same is probably true of fishing. Celebrating spring with sake beneath cherry blossoms, that is beautiful. But it's deceptive. Japan is a rough country.

Strictly speaking, Mari Ishikawa's rice neckpiece is in the tradition of the pearl necklace, which is erroneously called a necklace because it's a string rather than a necklace. The individual parts, pearls in the one case, here grains of rice, are threaded – that is, strung – one next to the other but are not concatenated at all. In Ishikawa's piece of jewellery, the 'strings' are intertwined and interwoven. This creates a sort of serpent, a strand, a fabric, a mesh. A fortuitous arrangement. Full of movement, a river. The grains of rice have forfeited their genuine virility. In favour of a picture that stands for cyclical life. Fragile, perishable, a coming and going.
The lustre of precious pearls is invoked yet a polished grain of rice also possesses a deep, silky sheen, a sophisticated translucidity and a subtly gradated palette.

How many grains of rice are many? As many as there are ravens on Narayama?

After Sissa ibn Dahir, also called Sessa or Zeta, had designed a board game with sixty-four squares (chaturanga, a forerunner of chess) for the Indian ruler Shihram (also known as Emperor Sheram), which greatly pleased Shihram, the emperor bade 'Sissasessazeta' to make a commensurate wish as his reward. Sissa ibn Dahir then expressed the wish that he should be given one grain of rice on the first square of the game board, two on the second square, four on the third and for each other square double the number of grains on the preceding one.[11] The king or emperor smiled and felt insulted by the Brahman's seeming modesty. Far from it. The emperor would have had to give Zeta, or whatever his name was, the world's entire rice harvest from more than 870 years. The story goes that the emperor was saved by the wisdom of his master arithmetician, who recommended that he count out the rice for Sissa ibn Dahir grain by grain.

Joseph Beuys pumped honey through the tubes of an installation. Fischli and Weiss formed miniature vehicles resembling cars from small Cervelat sausage links[12] for their photo work *Der Brand von Uster* [Uster Burning]. Dieter Roth built sculptures from chocolate. Daniel Spoerri launched an art movement of his own called *Eat Art* in the late 1960s. What all these examples have in common is that these artists, and innumerable others one could name here, have visibly made the unity of art and life the subject of their work by virtue of the fact that the consumption of all art also lies in eating (and drinking).

If this subject of existence and transmutation is transferred to the medium of jewellery, the images are consolidated by the proximity of the metaphor to the direct physical and spiritual process in the body of the person who is wearing the jewellery. Art and life are exaggerated here. The identification factor is raised to a higher power when art comes so close to getting under one's skin. The theme of the cyclical, of waxing and waning, also perishing, becomes ineluctable.

One of the three things I would take to a desert island is *Die Höhle des gelben Hundes* [The Cave of the Yellow Dog], a film by Byambasuren Davaa. This Mongolian docudrama is based on the idea of the eternal cosmic cycle. The main character, six-year-old Nansaa, confronts the question of reincarnation with childish logic. Riding wildly through the driving rain of a stormy night, she finds shelter in the yurt of a wise old woman and begs to know beyond all doubt whether she will be reborn as a human being in her next life.
'Come, I'll show you something.' The old woman makes Nansaa hold a pin with the tip pointing to the ceiling of the yurt and strews gently and slowly a handful of rice over the pin. *'Tell me if a grain of rice sticks to the pin.'* Nansaa: *'That's not possible.' 'See, my child, that is how difficult it is to be reborn as a human being and that is why a human life is so precious.'*[13]

Mari Ishikawa's rice jewellery was created in the thematic context of homeland. At that time Mari had already spent several years in Germany and did not have the money to visit Japan. Recollection and reality were overlaid and shifted. Mari Ishikawa put the finished neckpiece under the enlarger in the darkroom and made a photogram. What is so surprising about this confrontation of reality, imagination and image is that what emerged here is not, as is usually the case with this technique, an image that is entirely the opposite of reality but one that is virtually congruous with it.

The white grains of rice and the bright shiny silver wire also show up as a negative image against the black background in the photogram. Now, of course, without a shadow and seeming to hover. Is this the difference between reality and recollection?

Underway with Japanese friends in Ise Province. By train and on foot. We are looking for small, ancient shrines, originals, hidden in small forests. When a glade opens out, we cannot escape from the presence, the power, the humility, the clarity of those archaic places.
The surroundings are flat, rice as far as the eye can see. And then a rice field of a very special kind. It stands out, is spick and span and is solitary, at a distance from the rest. A sign explains that the rice grown here is produced for the Shinto Shrine in Ise. The field is enclosed by a low fence with a rice-straw cord, on which innumerable iridescent CDs flutter in the wind to scare off starlings and sparrows. A daily meal for the main shrine is cooked with this rice, following strict rules and very aesthetically. To feed the divine. A 'Bento Box' for God.[14]

'Eat up! Mari, eat up. In every grain of rice there's a god (Kami-san). You mustn't leave a single grain of rice uneaten. It must not be thrown out.'[15]

One last question: *'Mari, how many grains of rice have you in fact used for the neck piece?'*
'As many as are needed for a bowl of rice.'

Some days after Nansaa realised that she would probably never return to this earth as a human being, she was lying with her little brother on the scrubby Mongolian steppe. They observed the clouds and recognised with joyful certainty the reincarnation of a giraffe and, if I remember rightly, of an elephant, too.
'Have you ever seen a giraffe?' – 'No.'

Amid the oaks white dust was dancing: snow. *'Mama, you are lucky, it's snowing!'* Then he spoke the words of the ballad to himself: *'On the day on which she goes into the mountains ...'*[16]

1 Shichiro Fukazawa, *Narayama-bushiko. Schwierigkeiten beim Verständnis der Narayama-Lieder*, Frauenfeld 1998.
2 Ibid., p. 49.
3 Ibid., p. 11.
4 Ibid., p. 10, explanation: Hagi is a very beautiful plant that flowers in autumn and whose rosy blooms recall the shape of a grain of rice. This explains why the name White Hagi has been given to this valuable grain. Japanese cosmology imputes a divine power to rice, which is the ideal foodstuff. The term 'Mr' is an expression of the respect shown to it.
5 *Narayama* translates literally as 'the mountain with oaks'.
6 Shichiro Fukazawa 1998 (see n. 1), p. 10, explanation: the names of two wild flowers that are ubiquitous in Japan.
7 Ibid., p. 10.
8 Ibid., p. 51.
9 Ibid., p. 72.
10 *Yamato* can be translated as 'good relations', 'large community'.
11 The data online are diverse and very different. The names vary. The story is with grains of rice but can also be found with grains of wheat.
12 This is the name of a grill speciality in Switzerland that resembles cervelas de Lyon, Lyon sausage, but is, however, considerably shorter.
13 Inter alia, http://de.wikipedia.org/wiki/Die_Höhle_des_gelben_Hundes.
14 It is not (and cannot be here) my intention to introduce into this text the complexity of divinities in Shintoism and the relationship between Buddhism and Shintoism in Japan, which is also complex (but seems to function well). Apart from the fact that I understand so very little about it!
15 Mari's mother spoke like all mothers ...
16 Shichiro Fukazawa 1998 (see n. 1), pp. 74, 76.

CLOUD

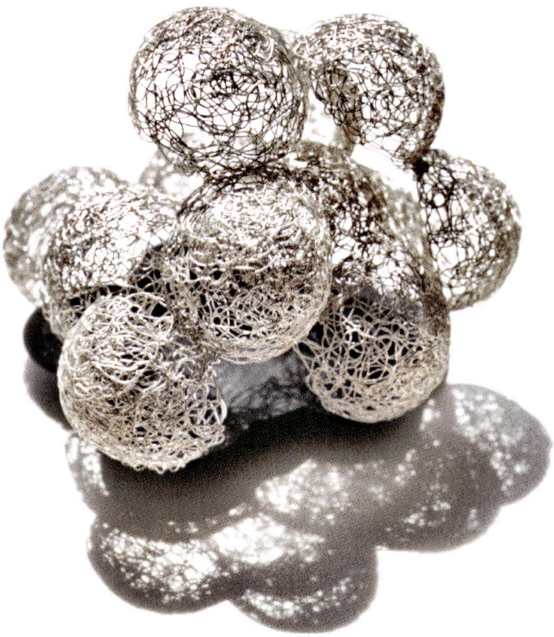

Brooch, 2002, 65 × 65 × 50 mm, 925 silver, partly oxidized

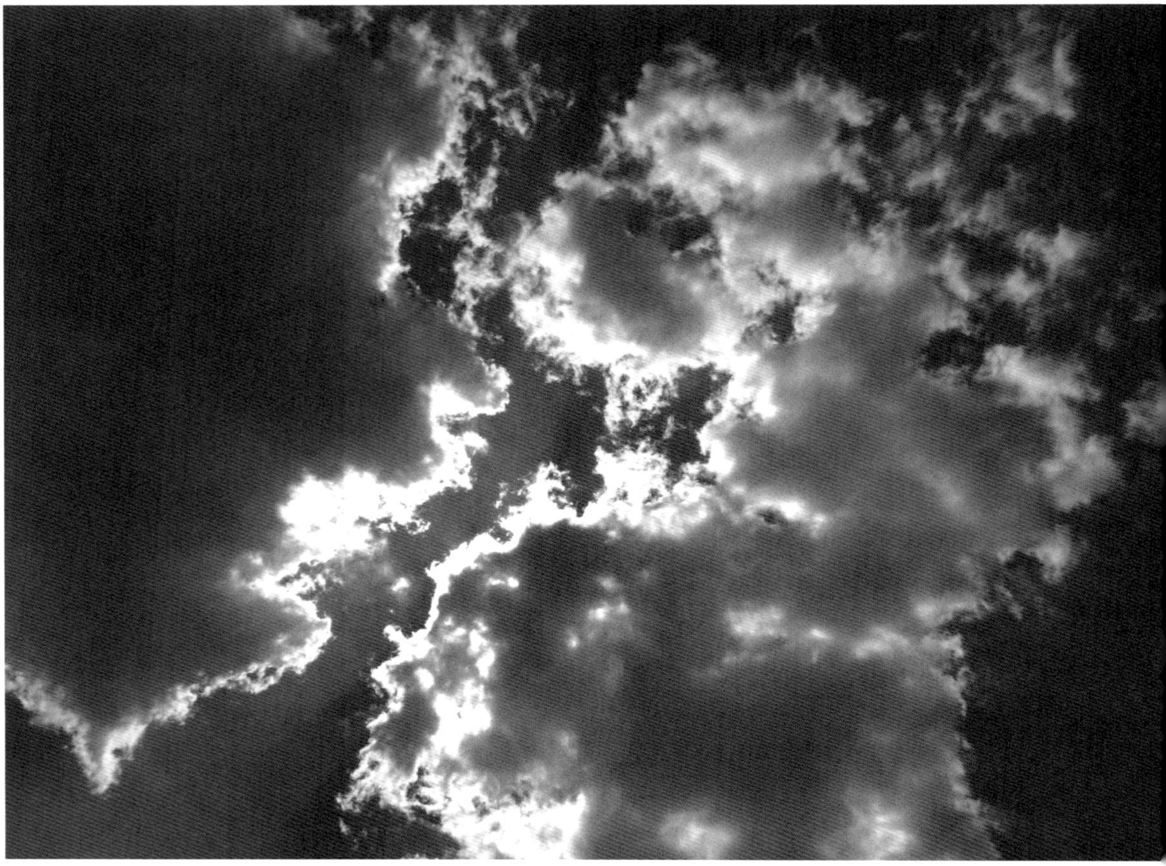
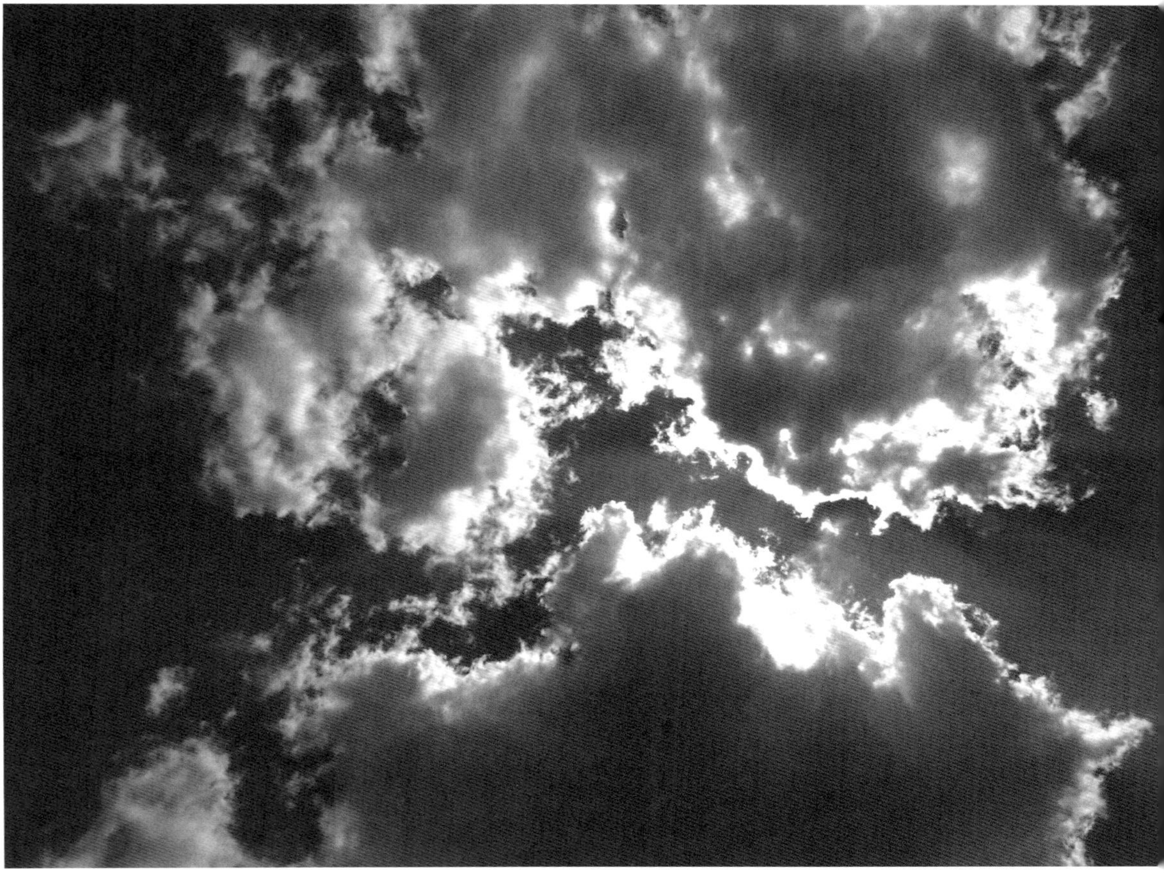

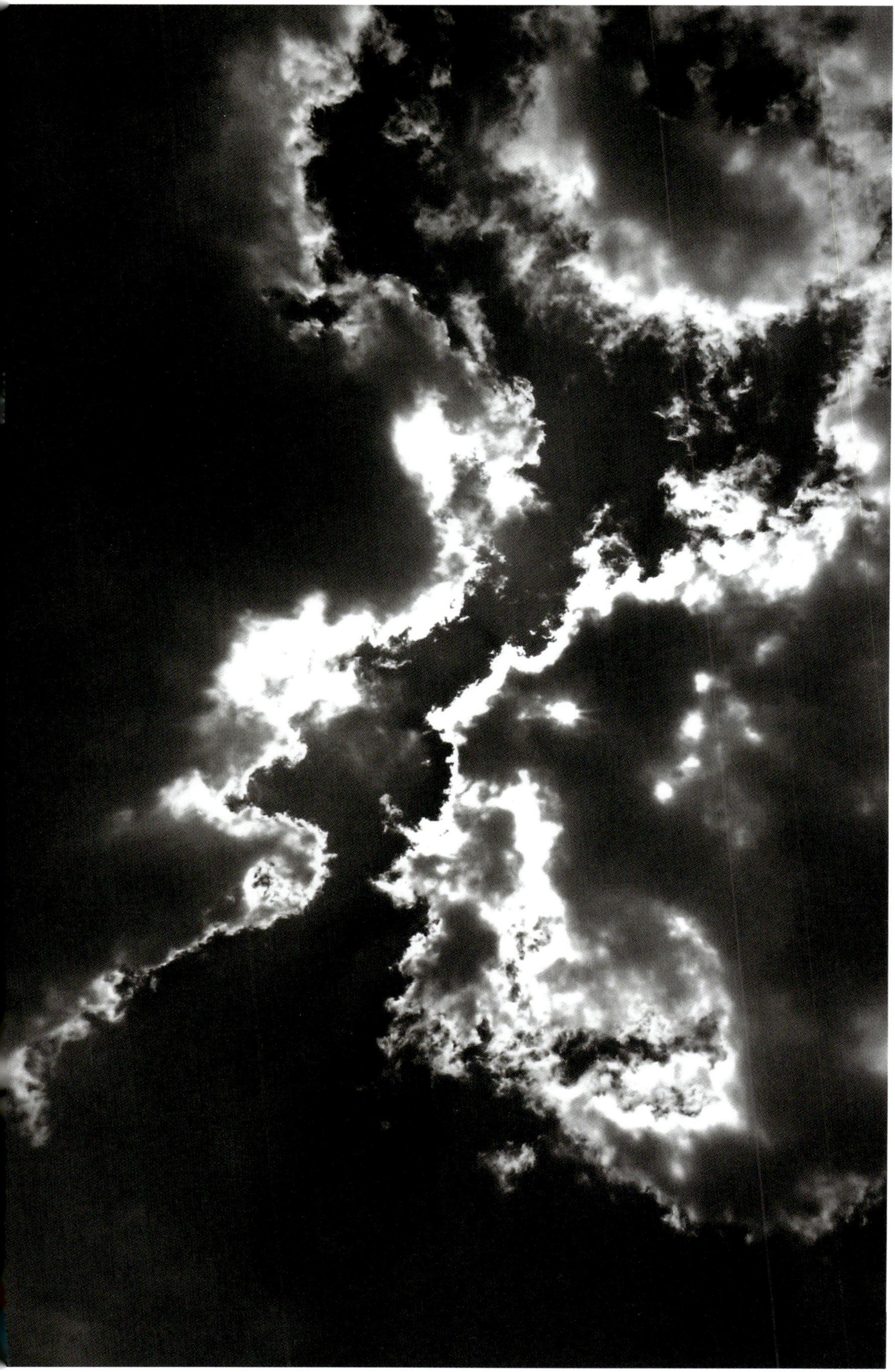

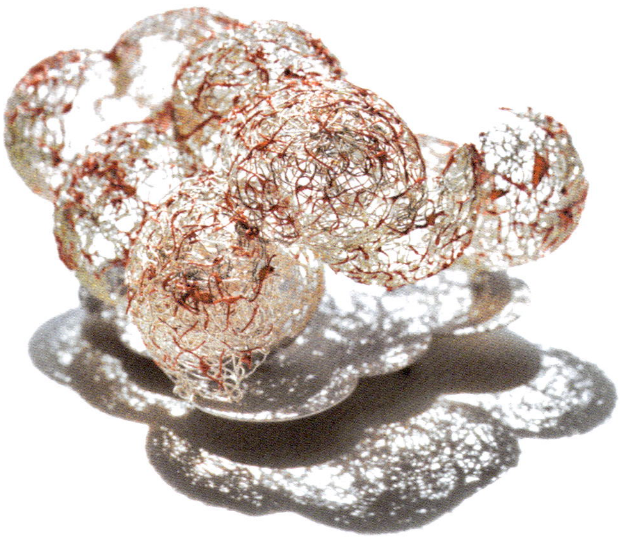

Brooch, 2002, 65 × 70 × 50 mm, 925 silver, Japanese lacquer

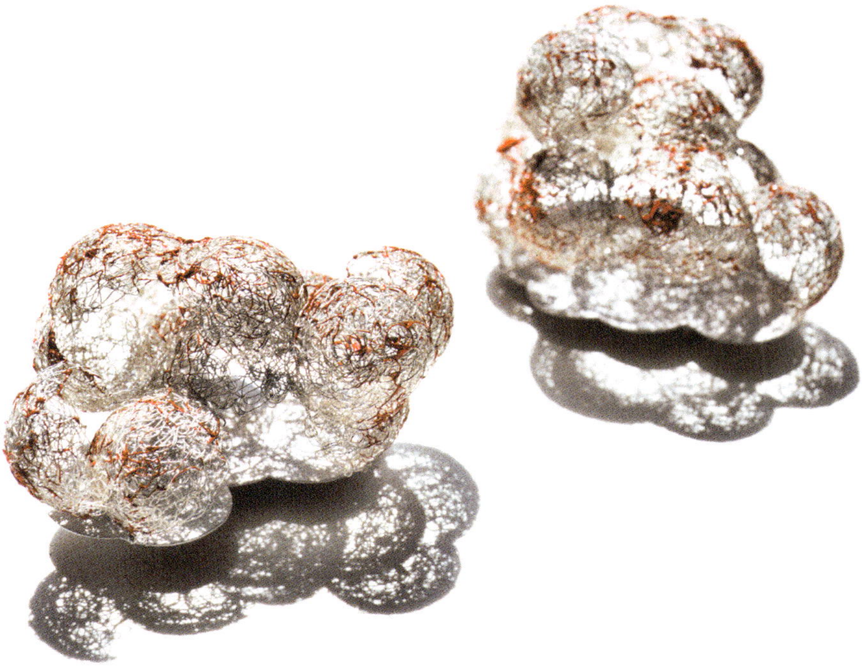

Brooches, 2002, L–R 65 × 60 × 50mm, 65 × 55 × 50 mm, 925 silver, Japanese lacquer

BLOOMING

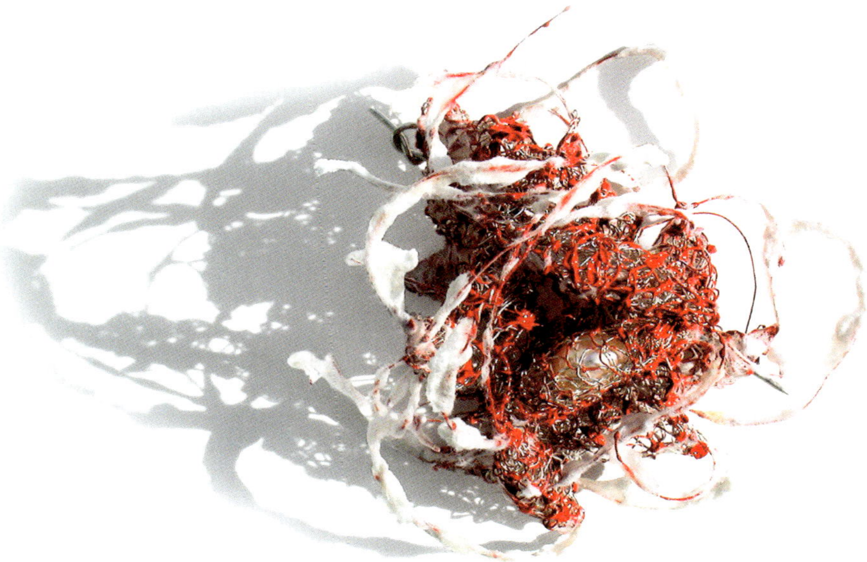

Brooch, 2004, 90 × 70 × 60 mm, 925 silver, Japanese Kozo paper, Japanese lacquer, Tahiti pearl

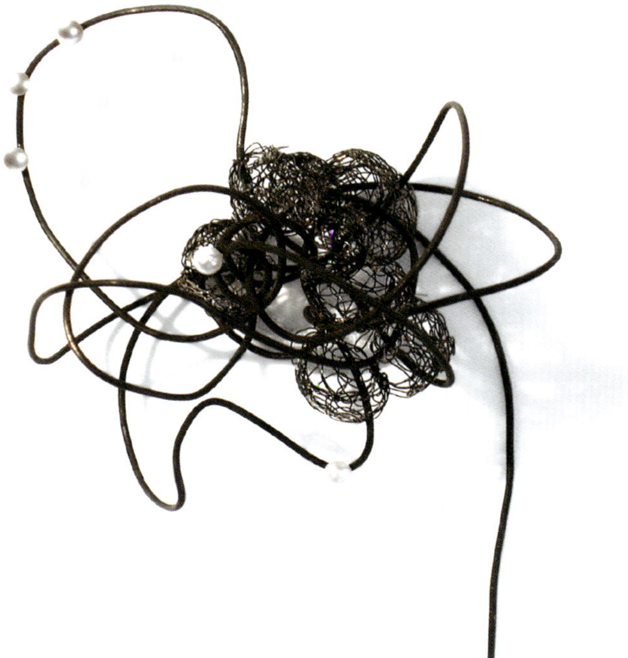

Brooch, 2004, 80 × 50 × 40 mm, 925 silver, oxidized, pearls

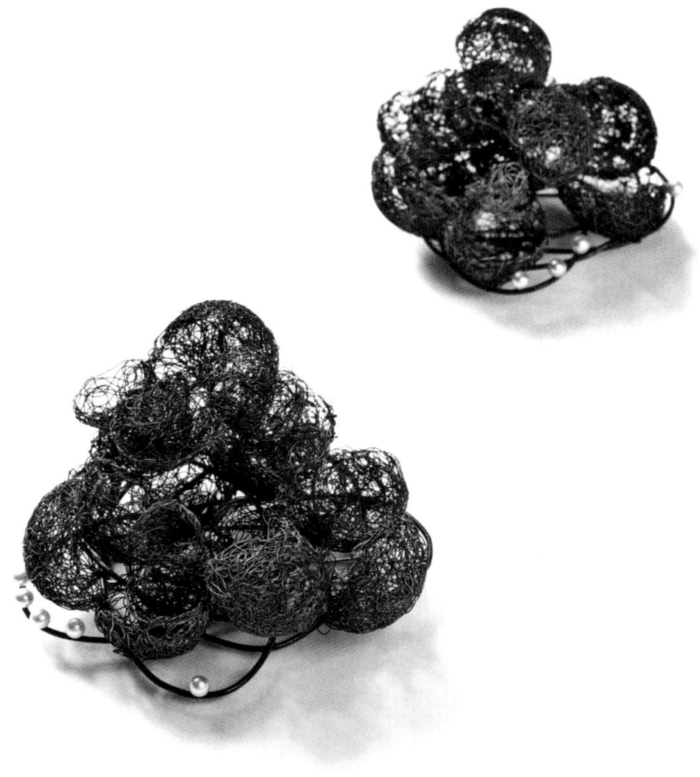

Brooches, 2004, L–R 65 × 65 × 40 mm, 55 × 60 × 45 mm, 925 silver, oxidized, pearls

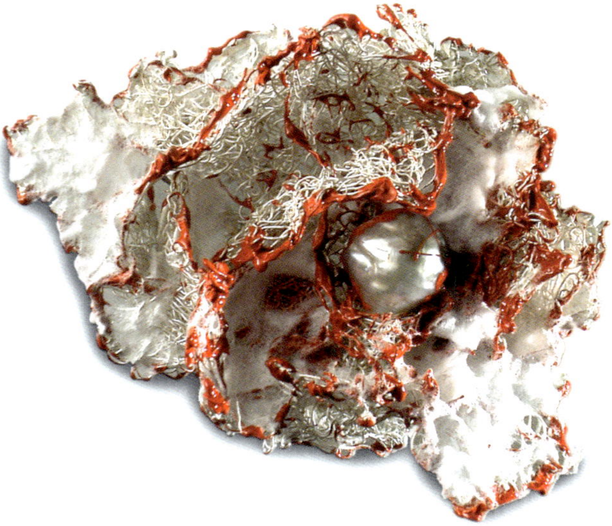

Brooch, 2004, 80 × 65 × 30 mm, 925 silver, Japanese Kozo paper, Japanese lacquer, Tahiti pearl

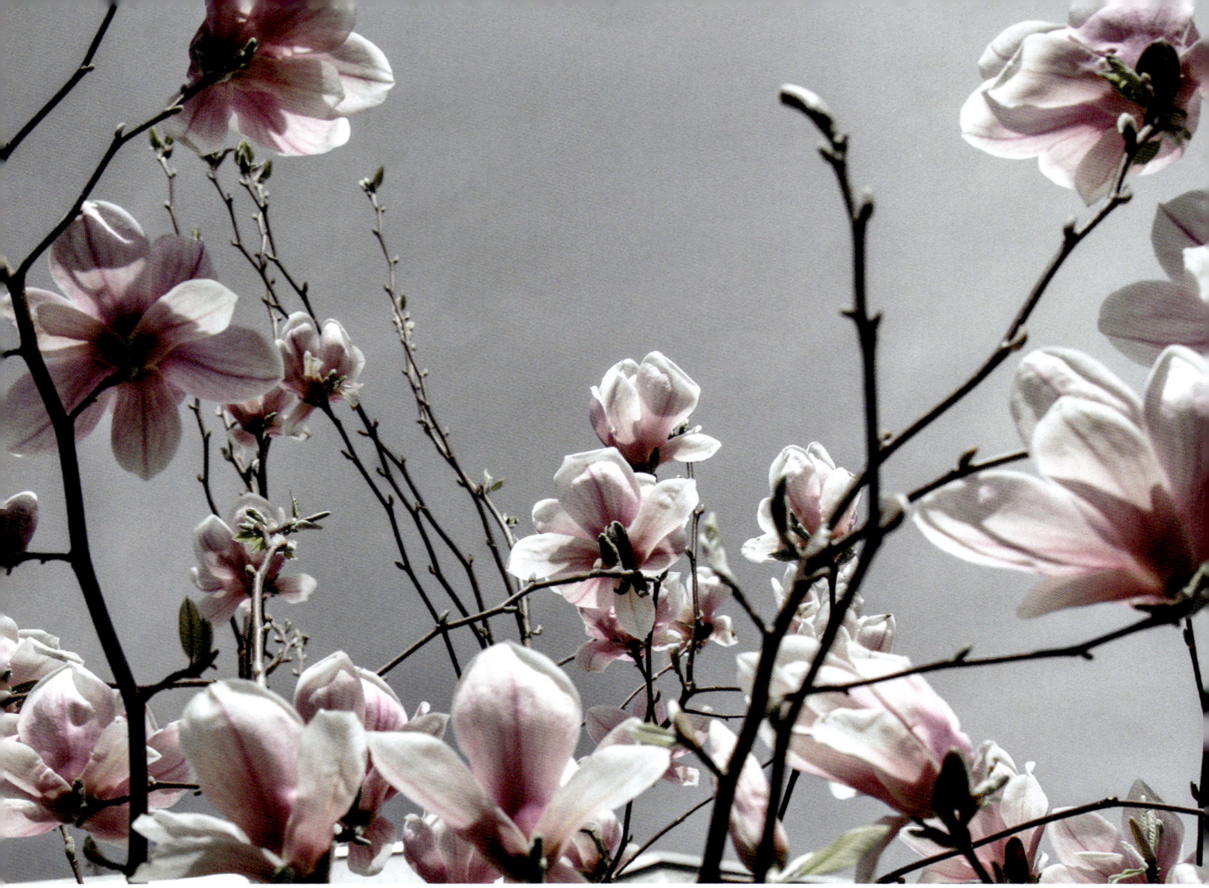

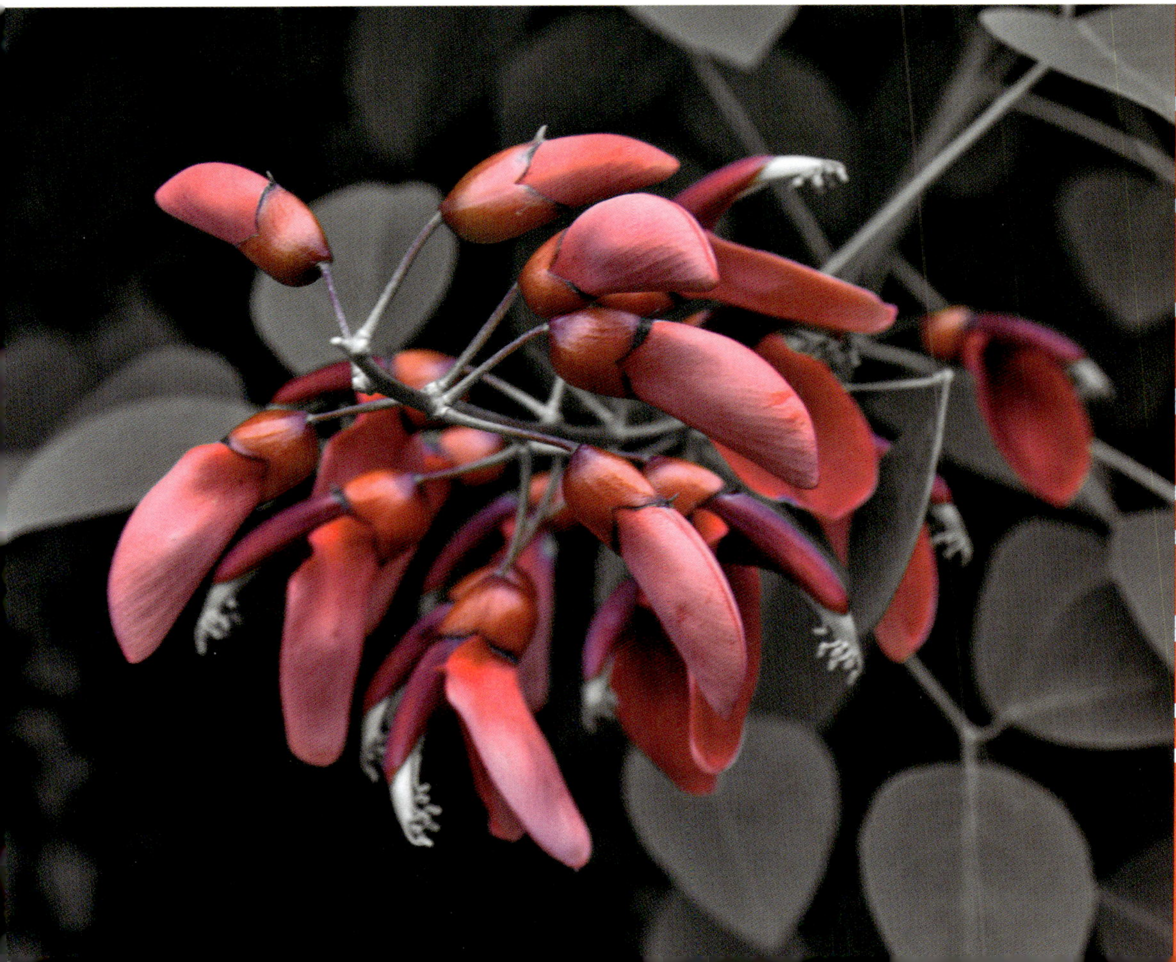

IN THE SHADE OF THE TREE

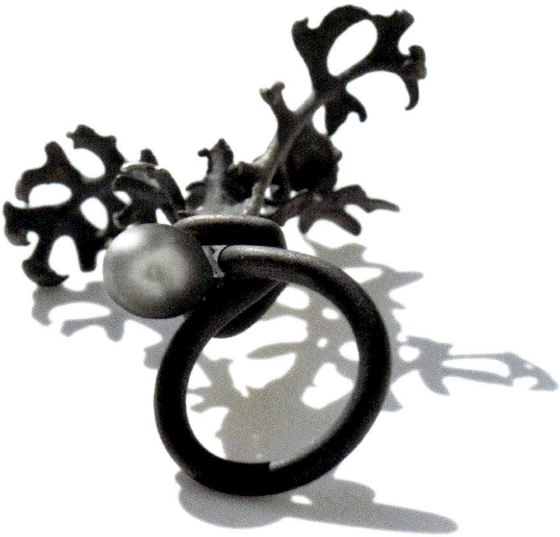

Ring, 2007, 70 × 50 × 30 mm, 925 silver, oxidized, Tahiti pearl

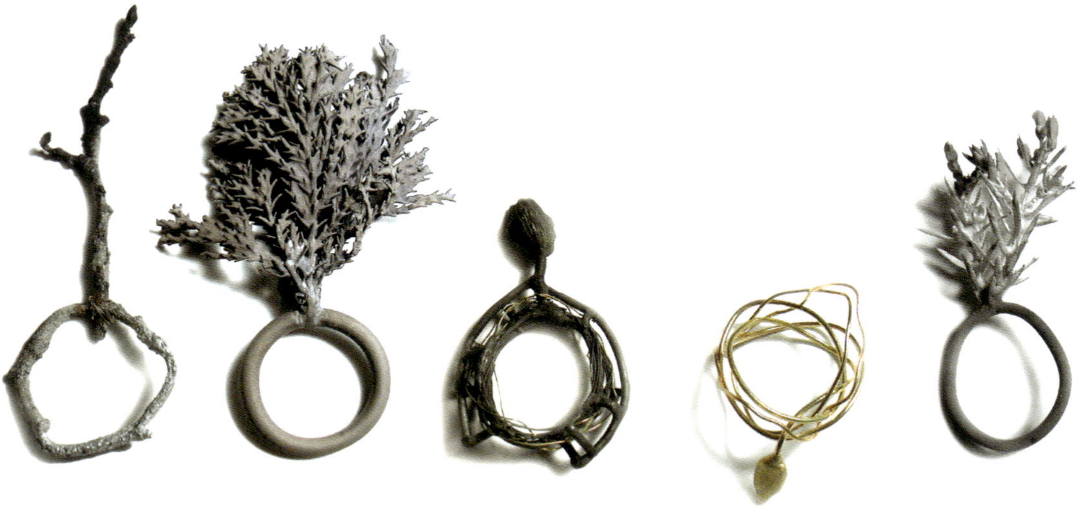

Rings, 2006, L–R 70 × 35 × 15 mm, 65 × 45 × 10 mm, 40 × 30 × 15 mm, 40 × 30 × 20 mm, 60 × 45 × 15 mm,
750 gold, 925 silver, oxidized

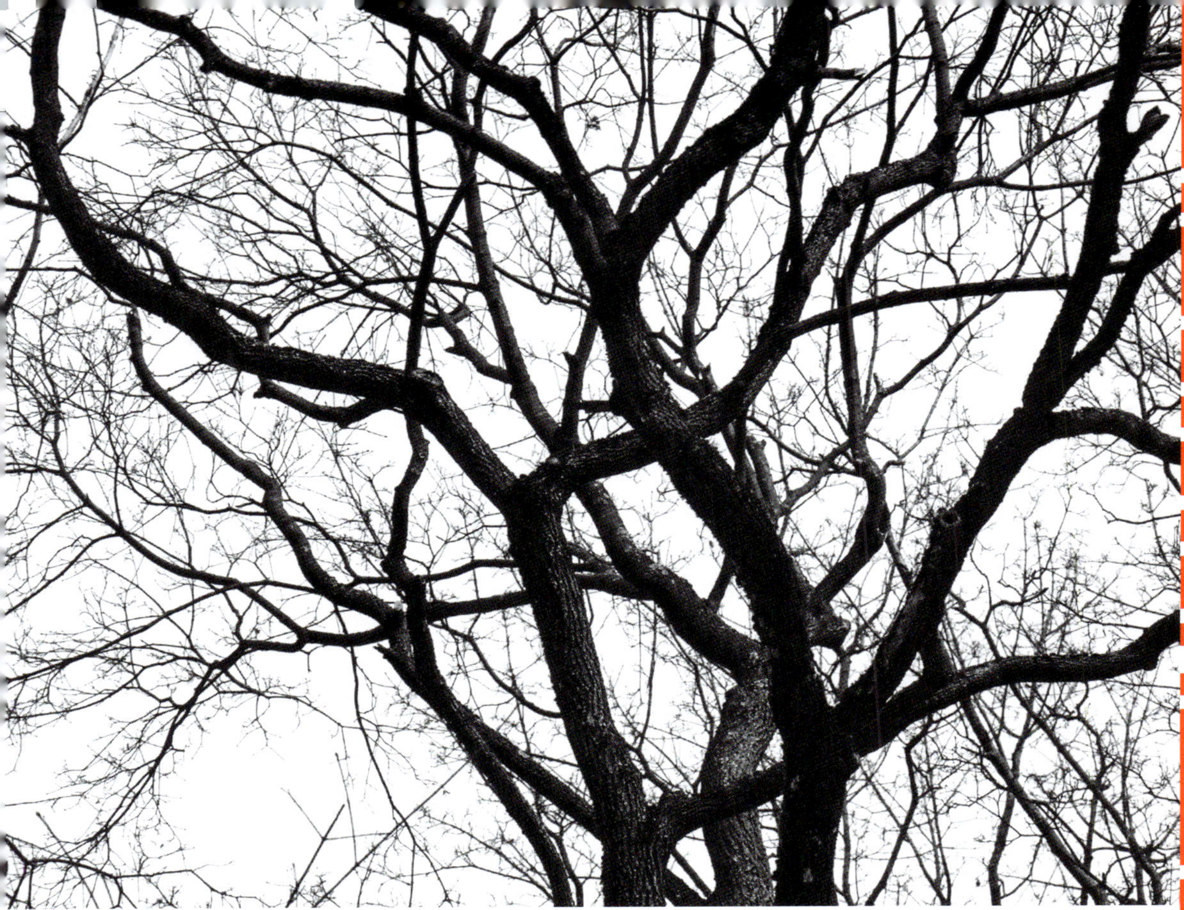

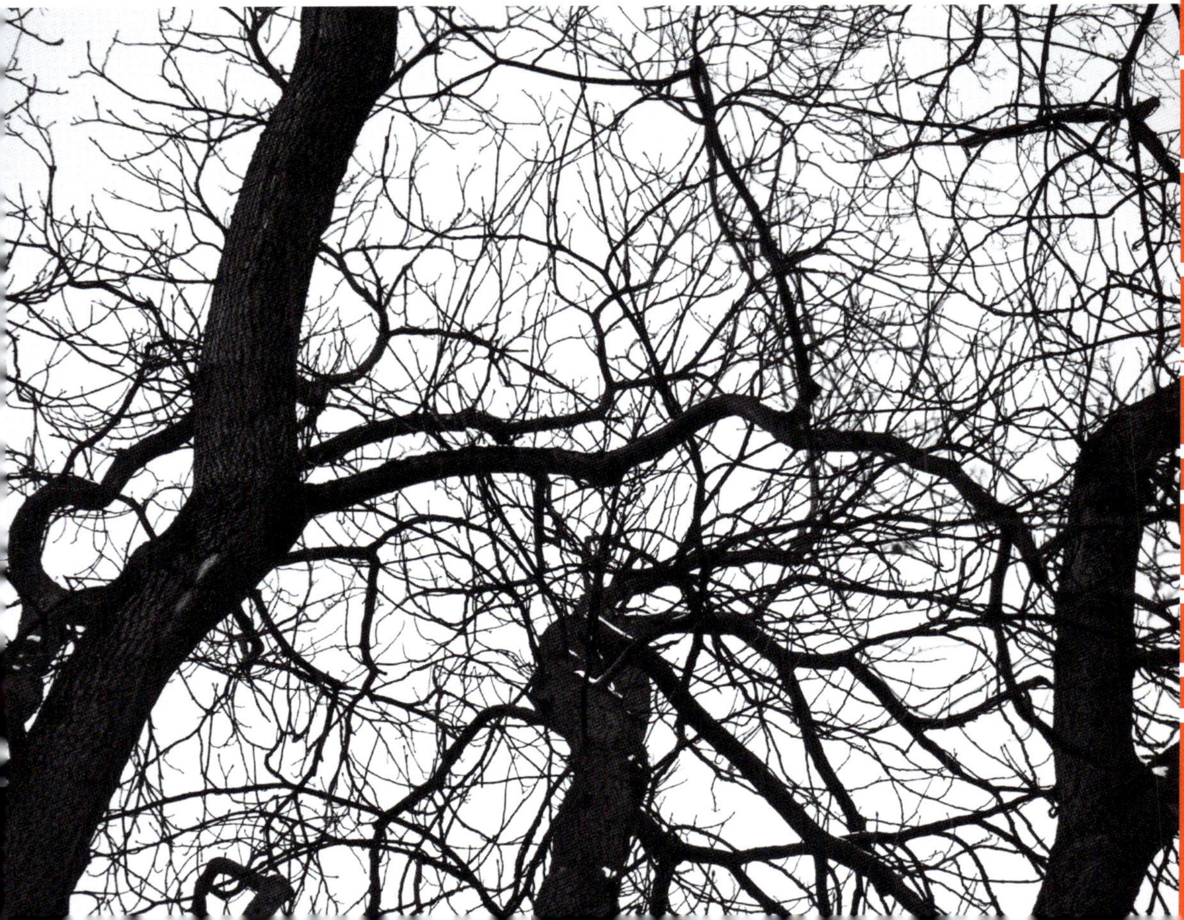

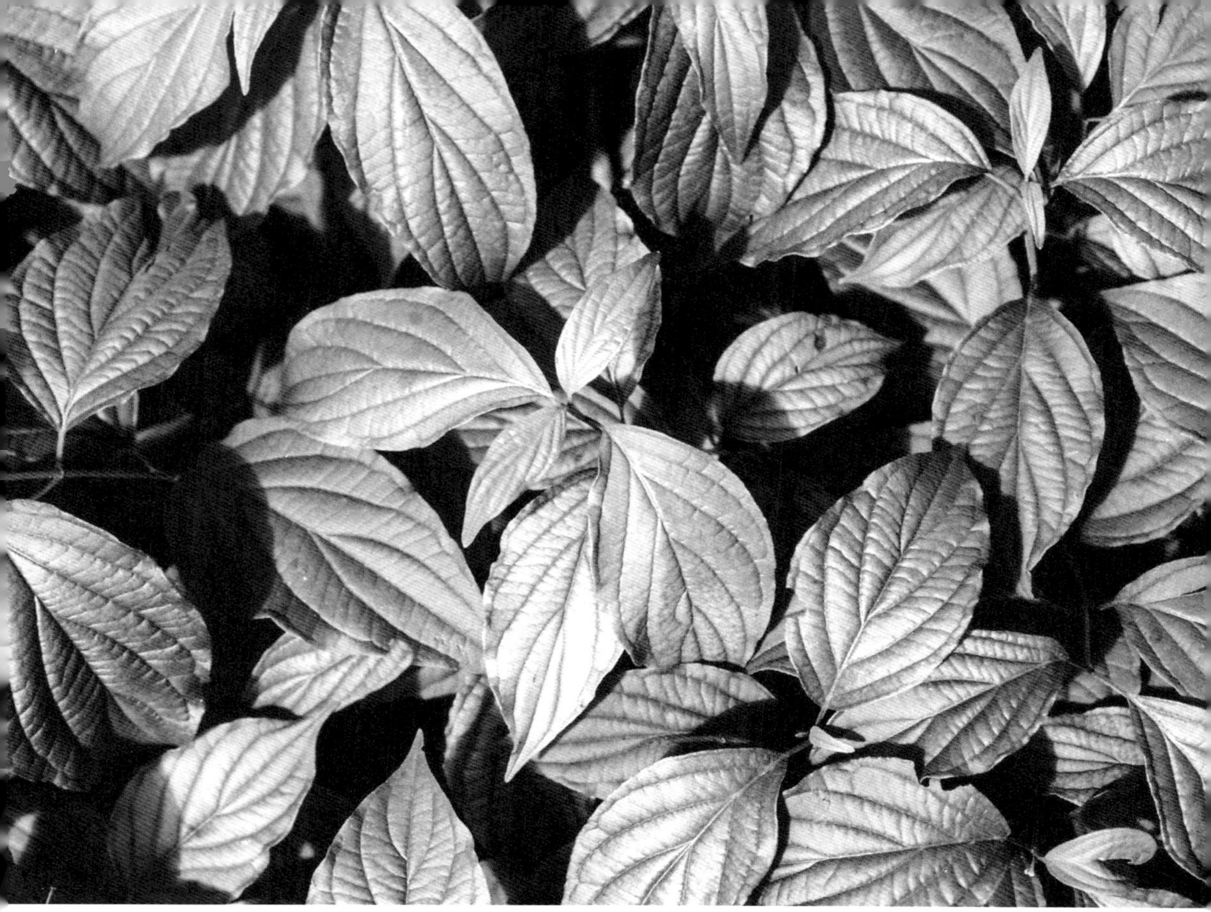

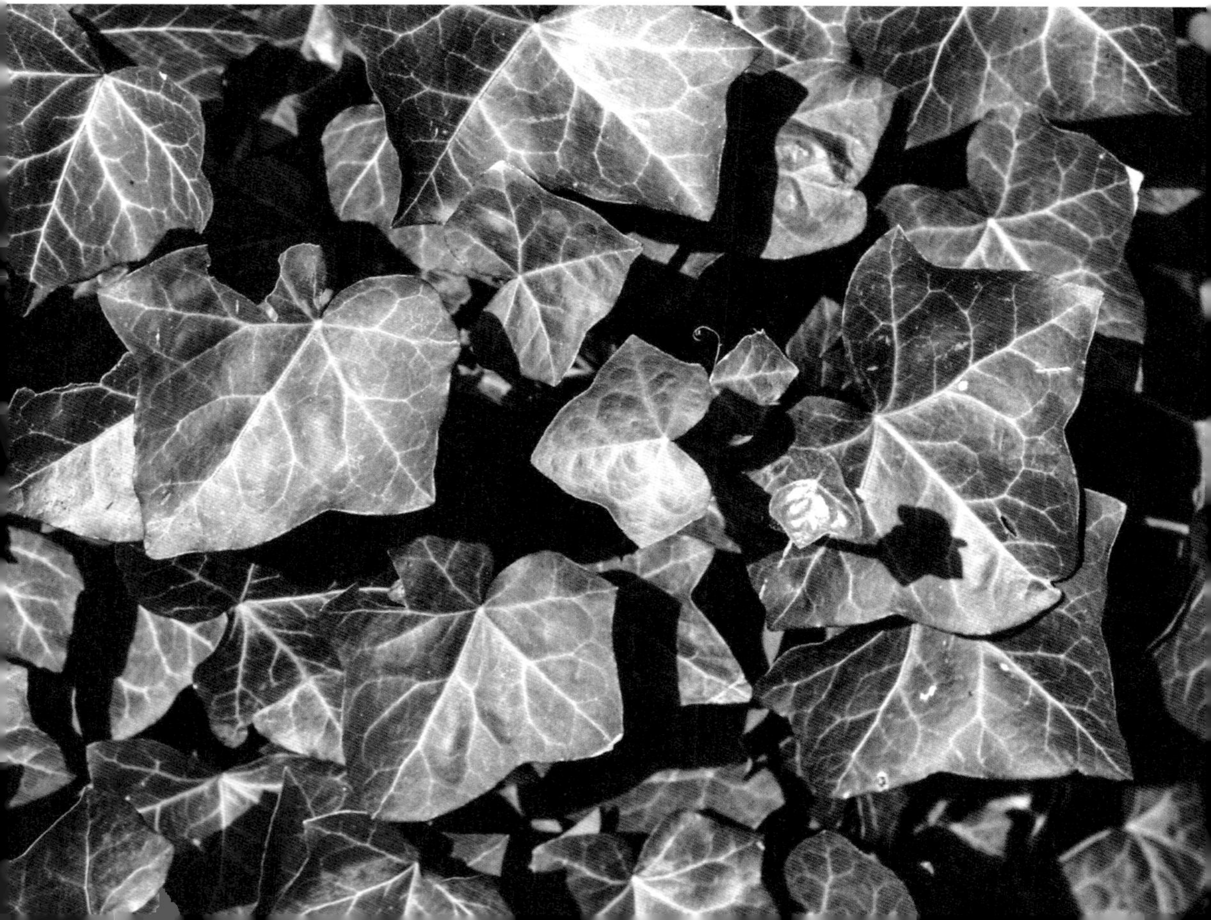

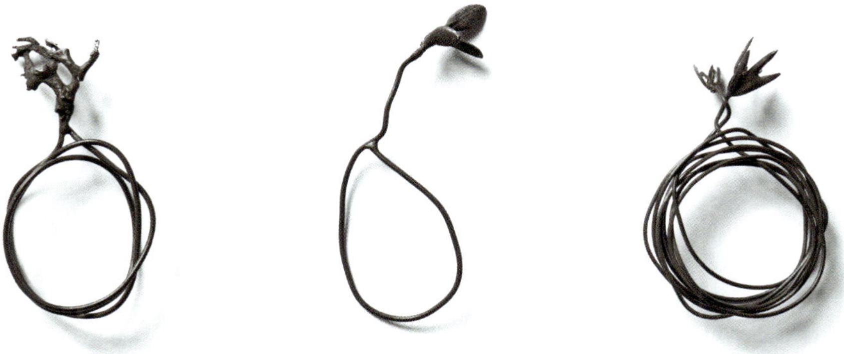

Rings, 2011. L–R 40 × 20 × 10 mm, 50 × 25 × 10 mm, 40 × 25 × 10 mm, 925 silver, oxidized

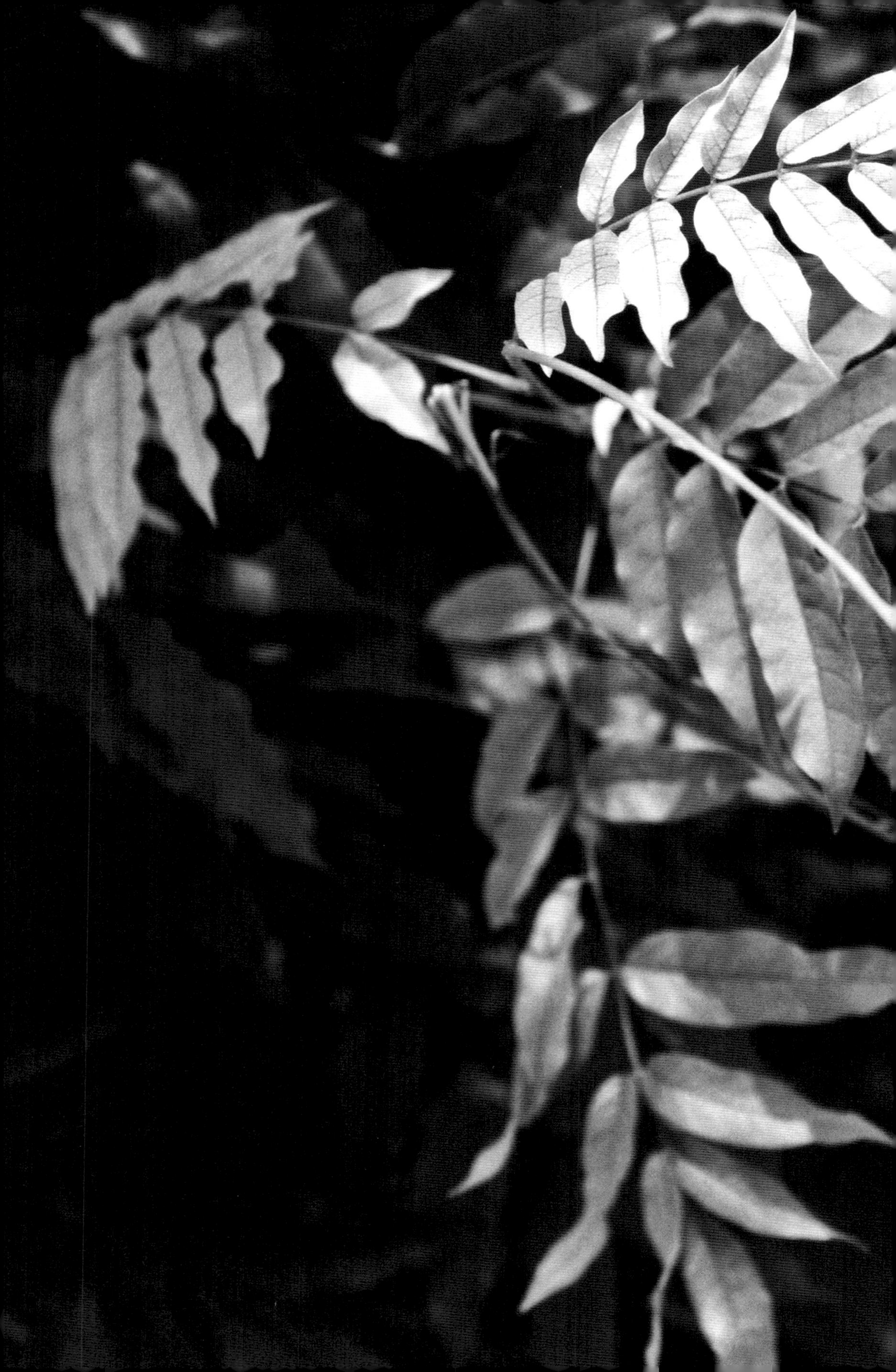

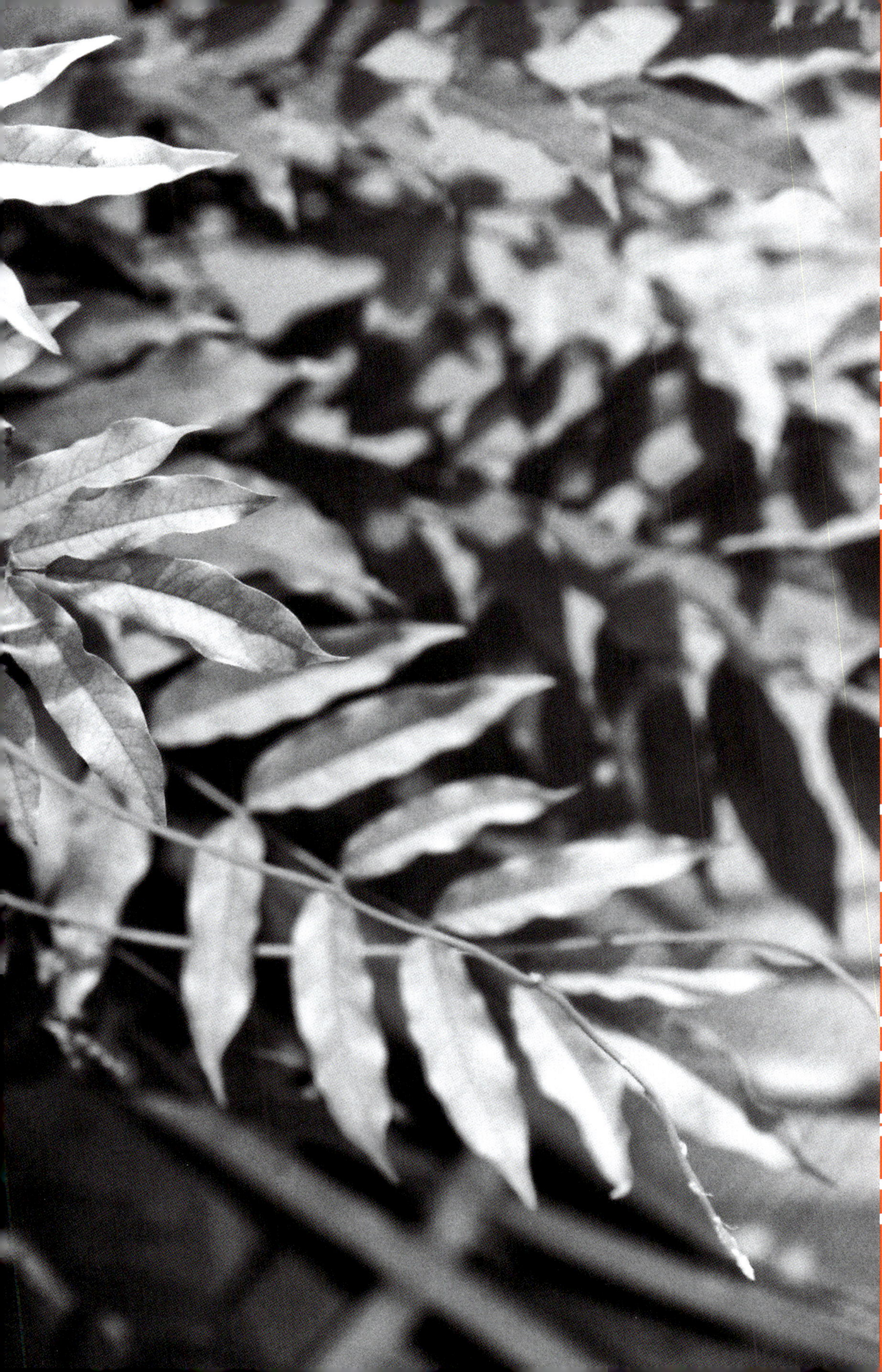

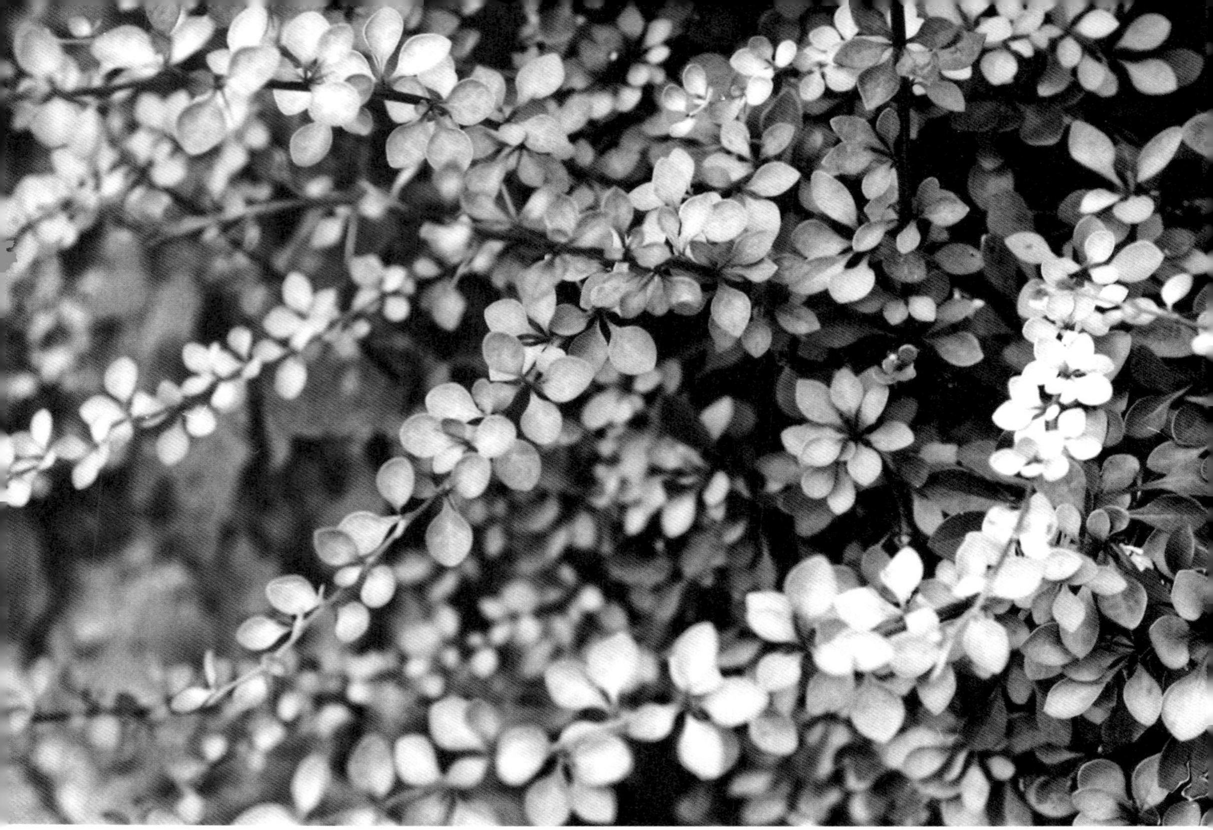

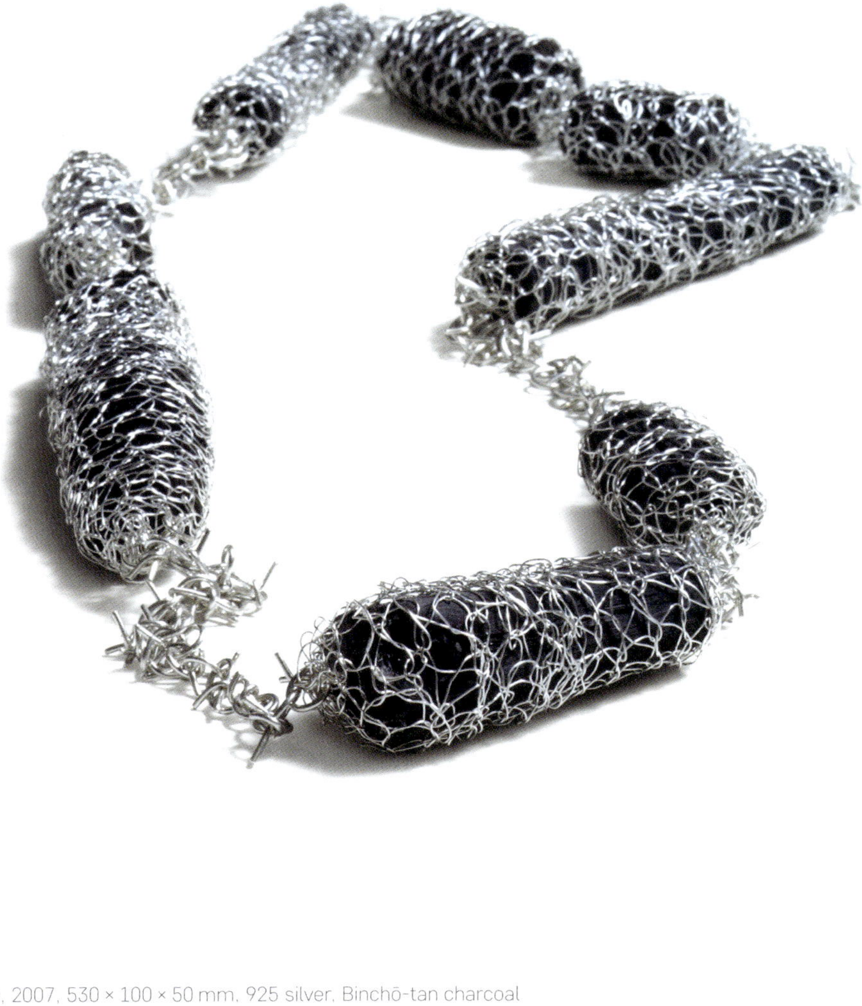

Neckpiece, 2007, 530 × 100 × 50 mm, 925 silver, Binchō-tan charcoal

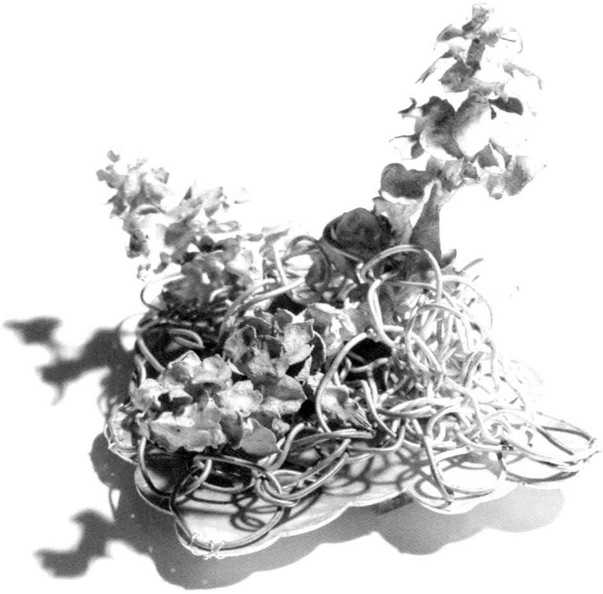

Brooch. 2006. 60 × 45 × 50 mm. 925 silver

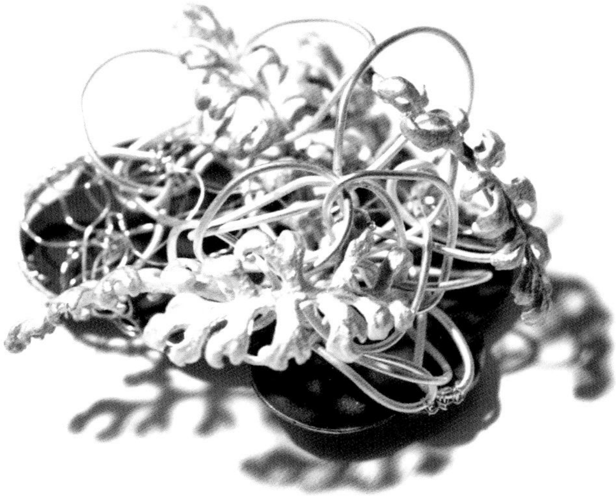

Brooch, 2007, 70 × 60 × 40 mm, 925 silver, partly oxidized

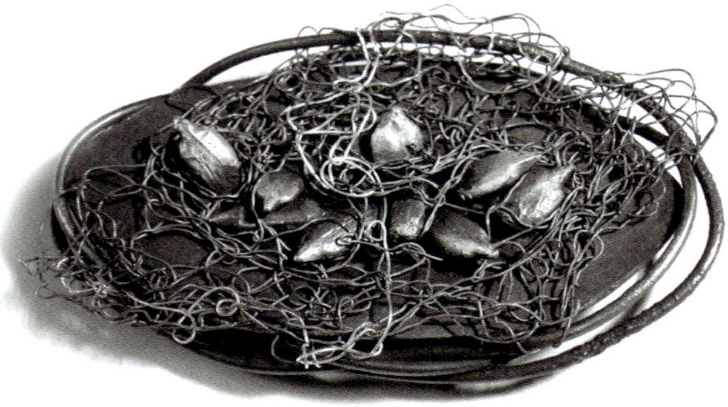

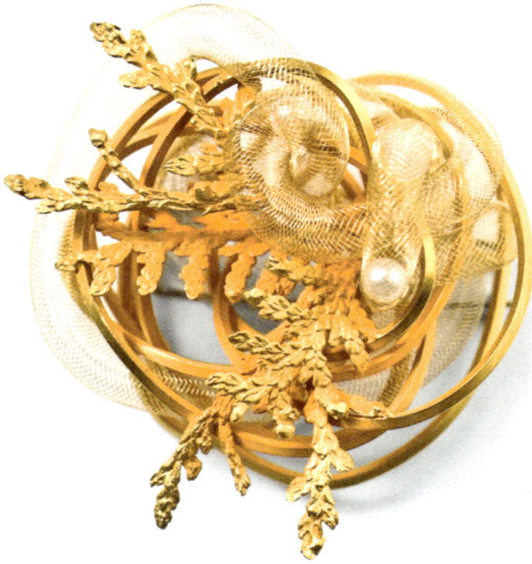

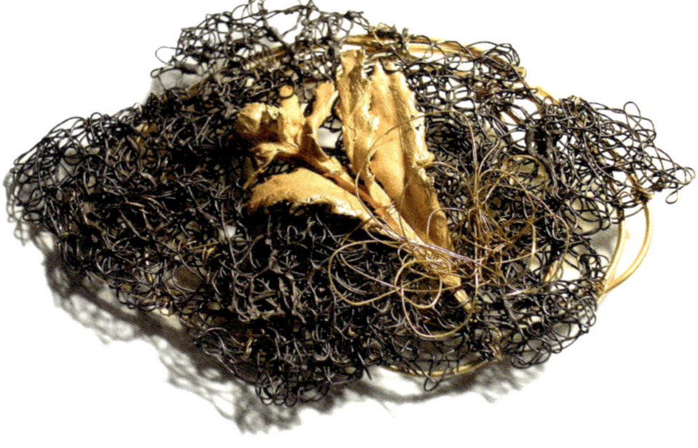

Brooches. 2006, T–B 70 × 45 × 15 mm. 925 silver, oxidized; 2007, 70 × 85 × 60 mm, 750 gold, 925 silver, gold-plated, pearl; 2006, 90 × 50 × 15 mm, 750 gold, 925 silver, gold-plated, 925 silver, oxidized

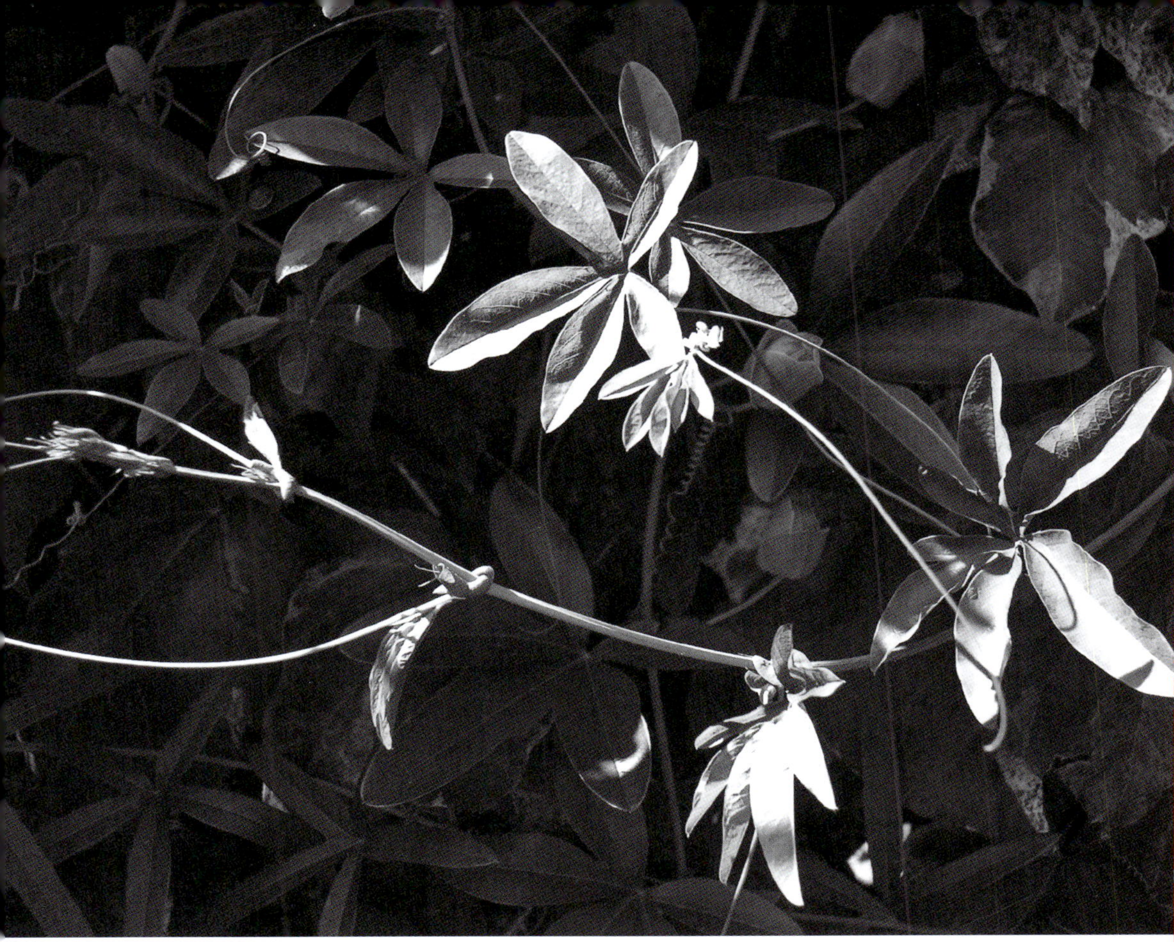

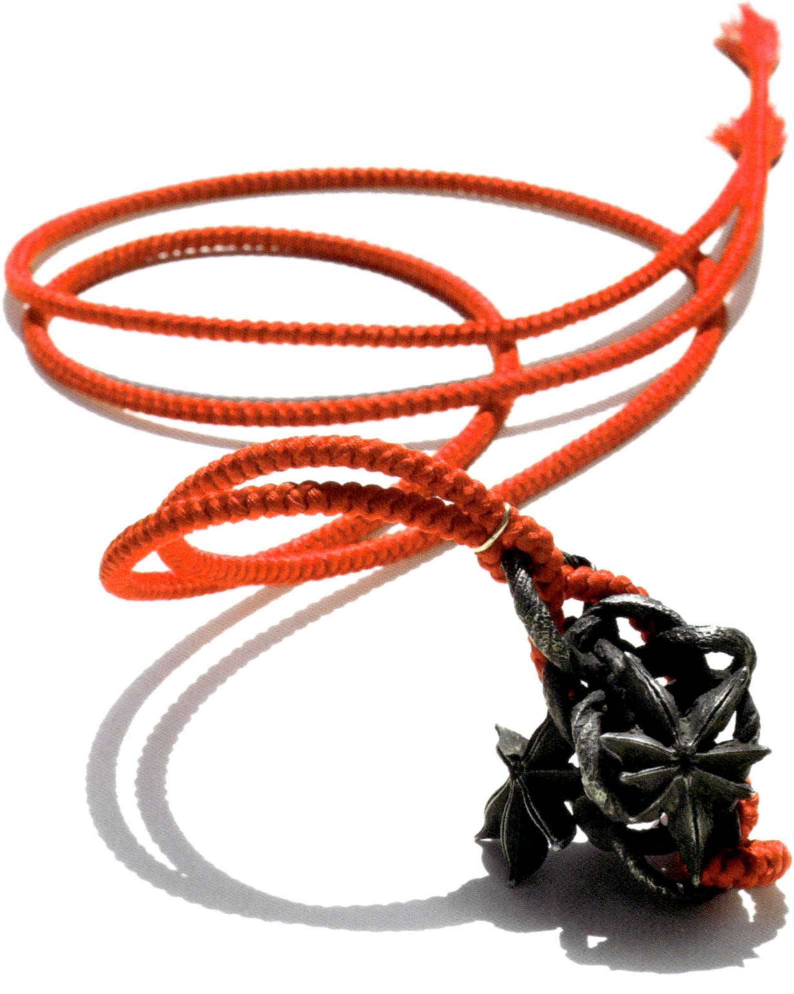

Neckpiece. 2007. 1.000 mm long. 750 gold. 925 silver, oxidized. silk

MOONLIGHT SHADOW

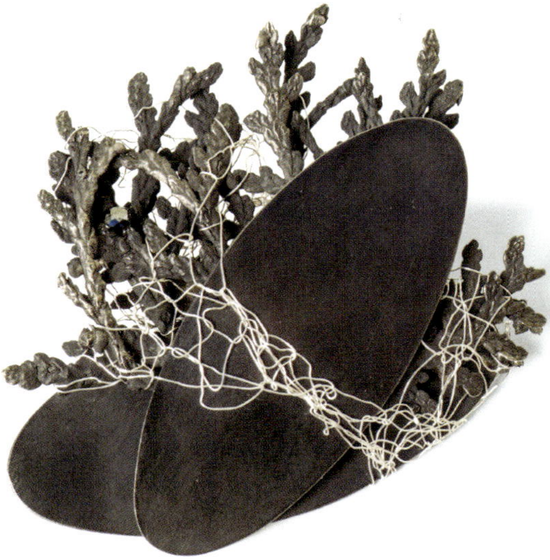

Brooch, 2008, 65 × 75 × 40 mm, 925 silver, partly oxidized, black diamond

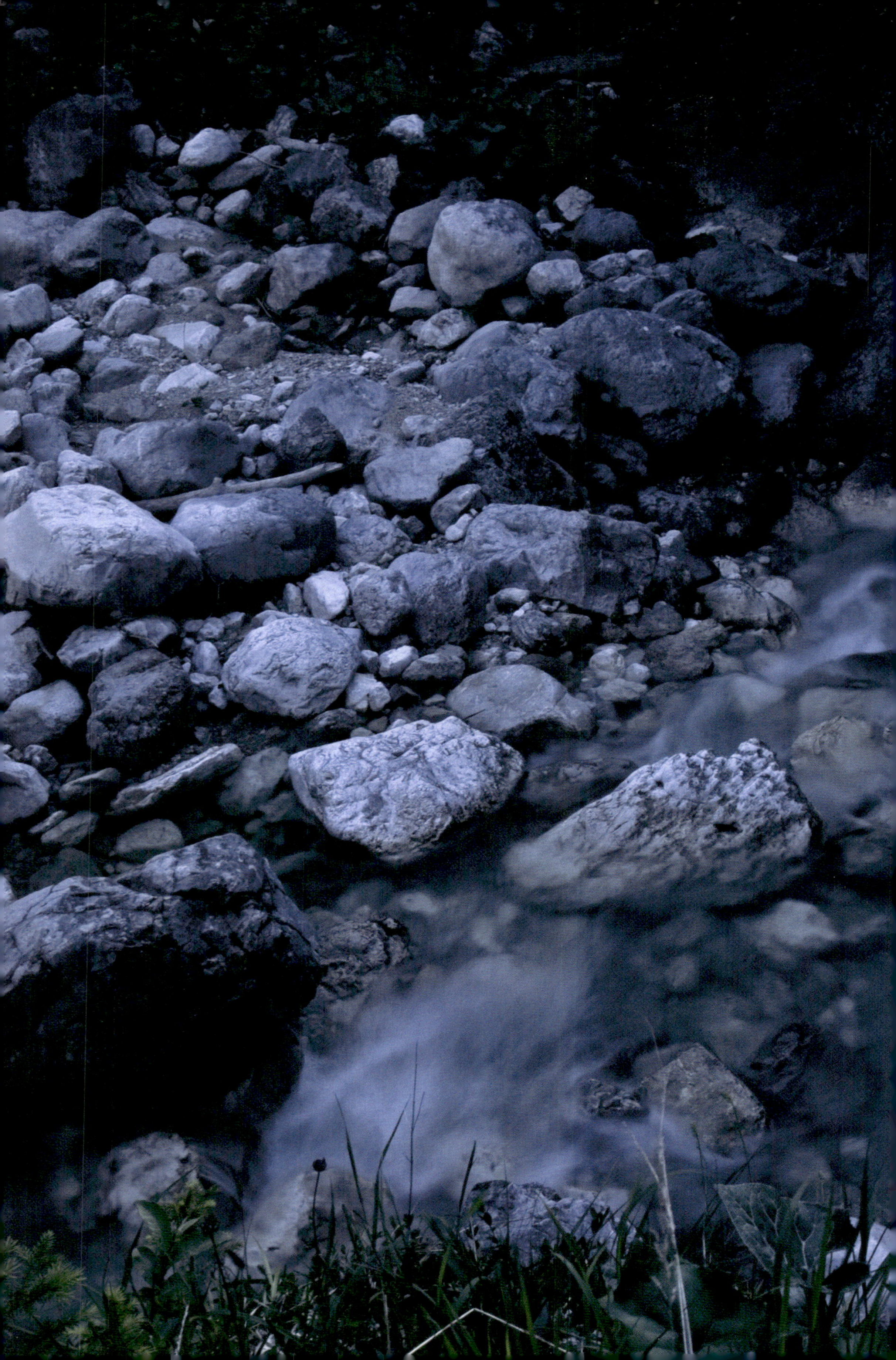

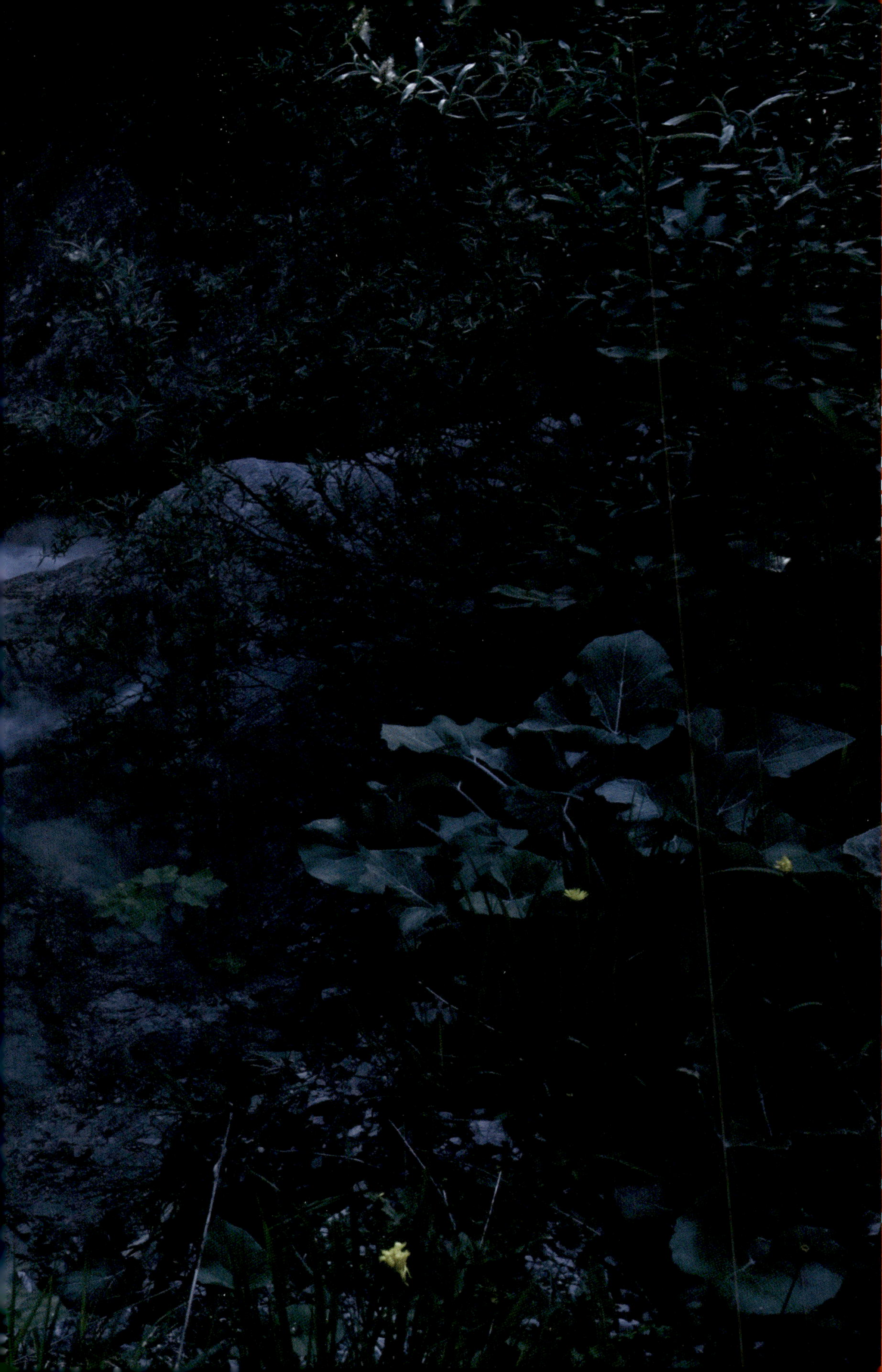

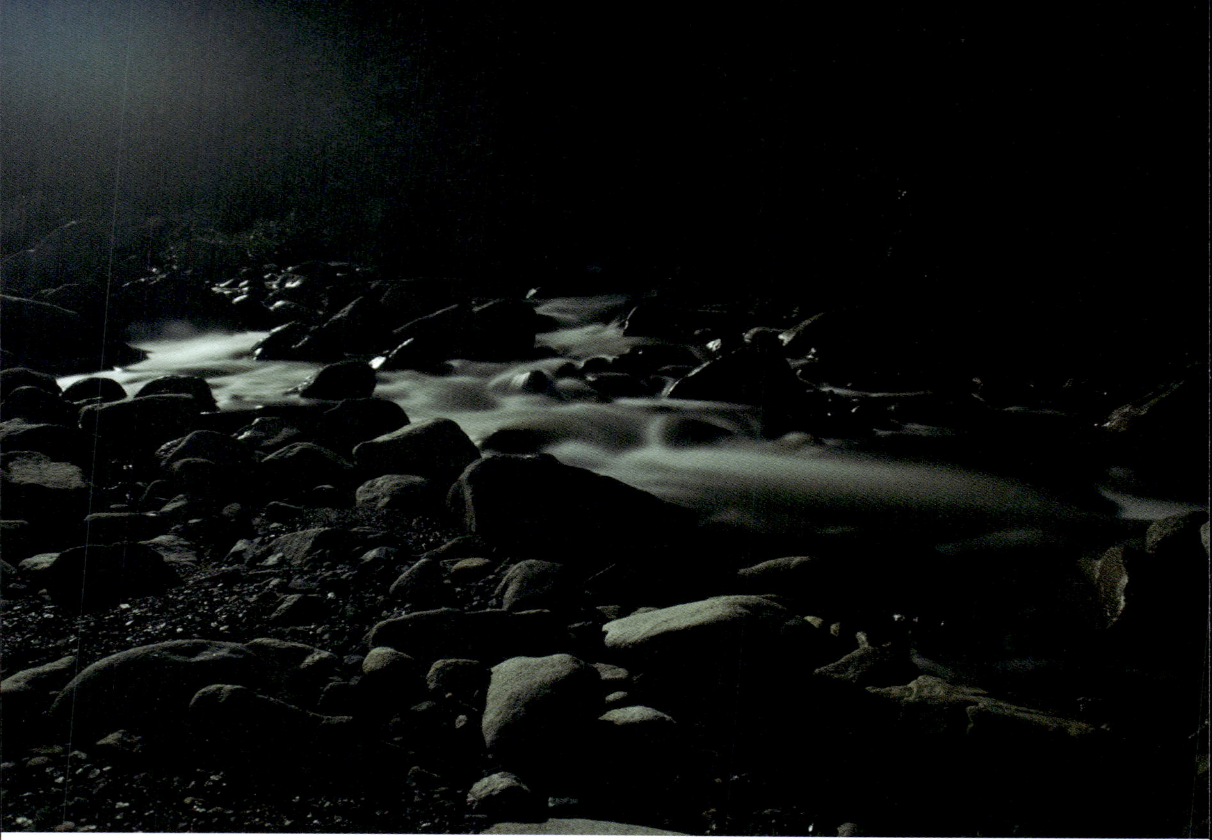

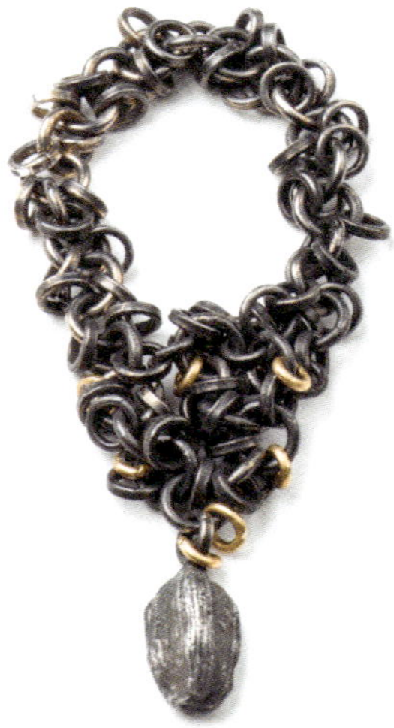

Ring, 2008, 50 × 30 × 10 mm, 750 gold, 925 silver, oxidized
Page 63: Ring, 2007, 75 × 55 × 70 mm, 750 gold, 925 silver, oxidized

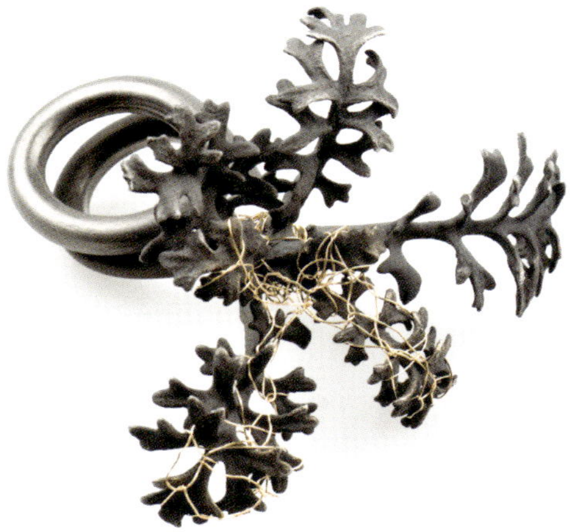

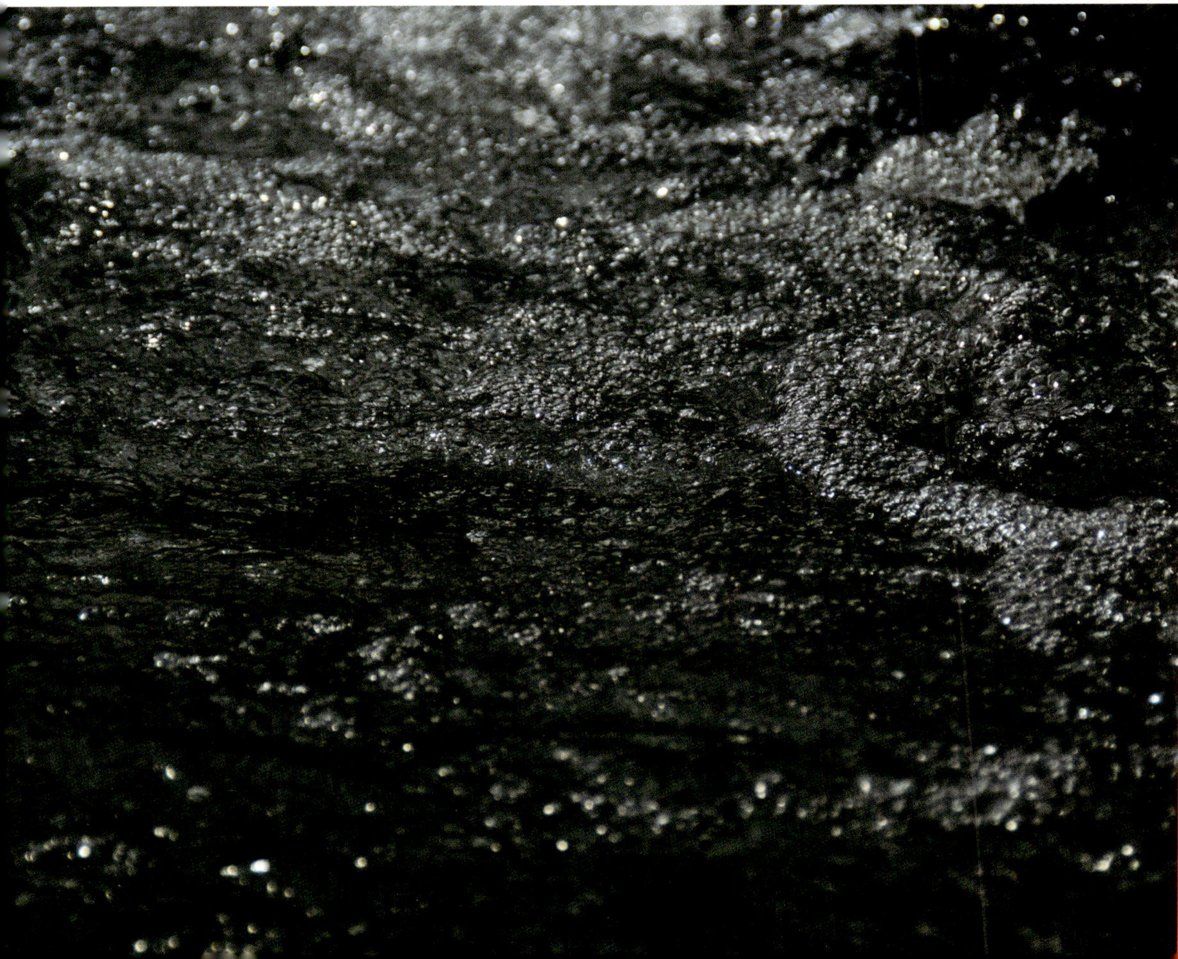

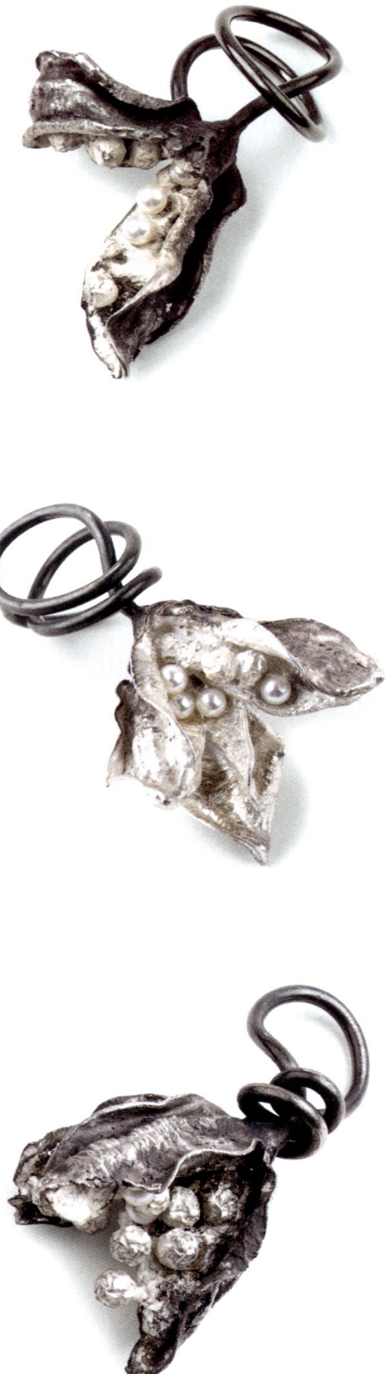

Rings, 2009–2010, T–B 70 × 50 × 25 mm, 80 × 55 × 35 mm, 75 × 45 × 45 mm, 925 silver, partly oxidized, pearls

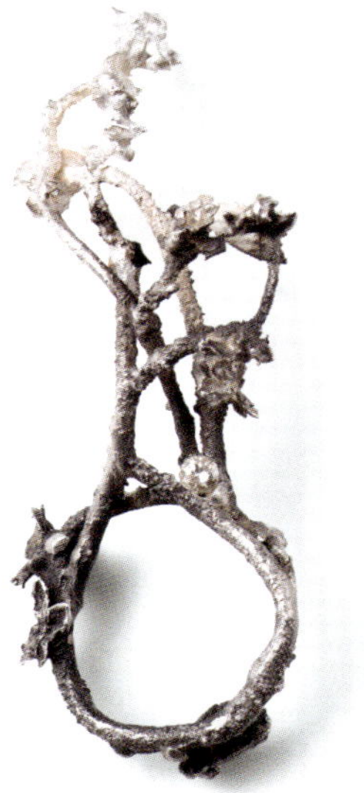

Ring, 2009, 75 × 30 × 30 mm, 925 silver, partly oxidized, diamond

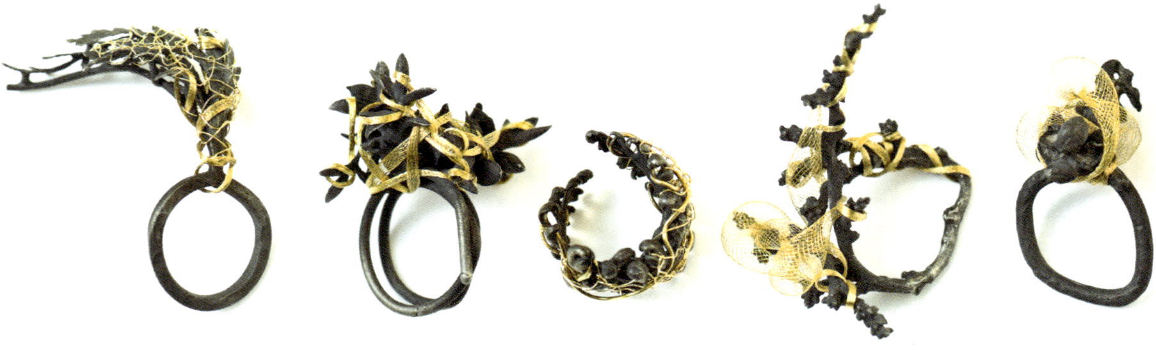

Rings, 2007–2008. L–R 60 × 50 × 20 mm, 45 × 35 × 55 mm, 30 × 30 × 25 mm, 45 × 55 × 55 mm, 40 × 30 × 20 mm, 750 gold, 925 silver, oxidized

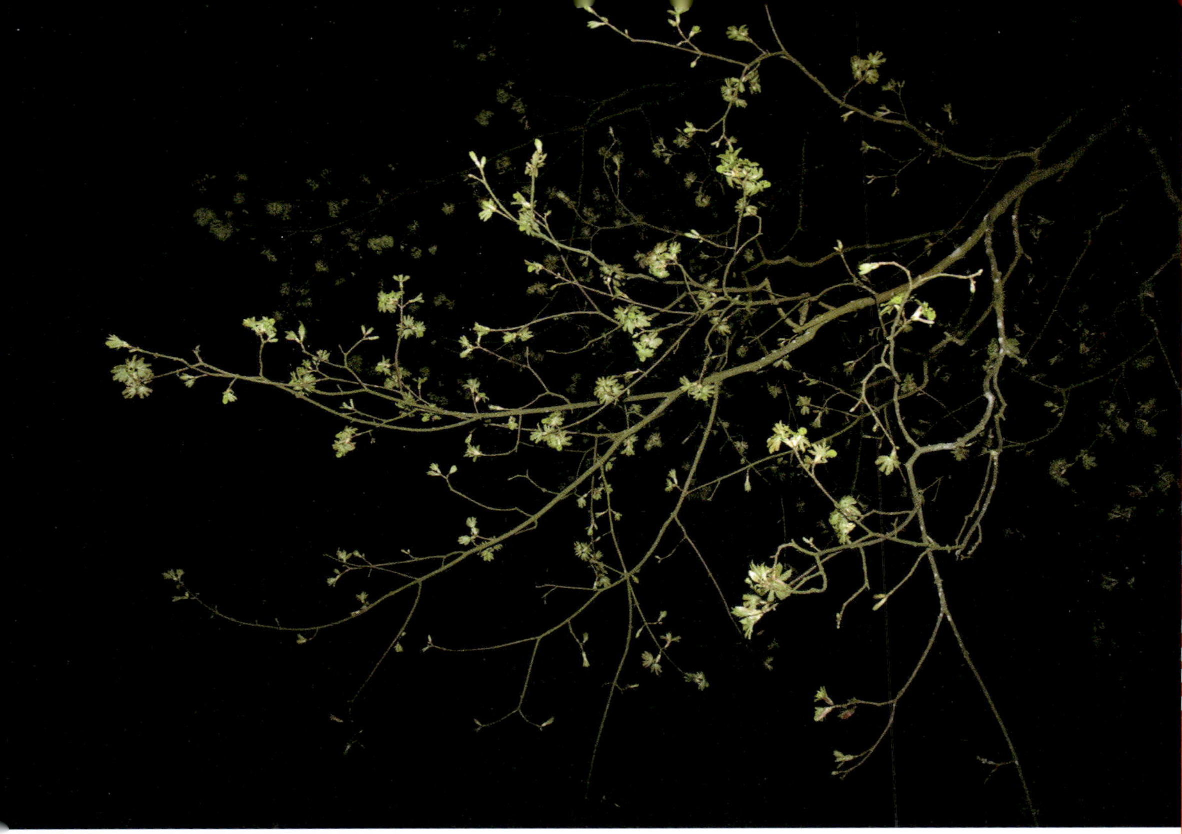

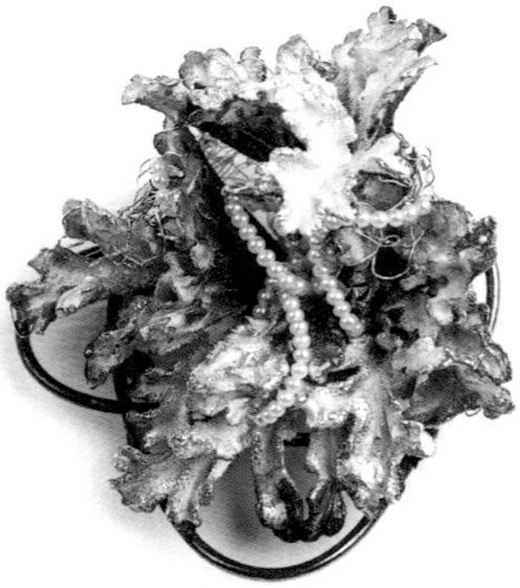

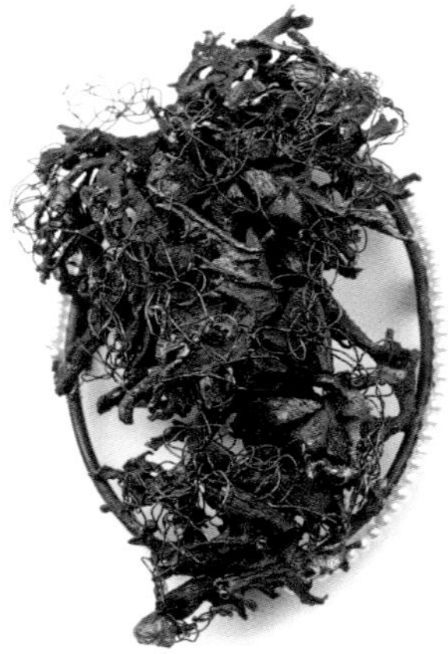

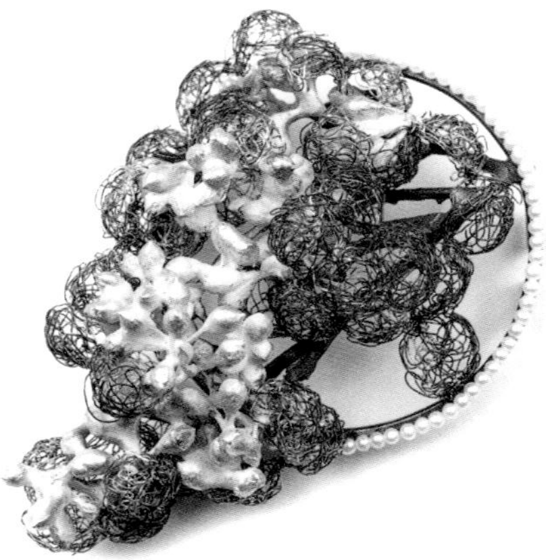

Brooches, T–B 2010, 50 × 55 × 50 mm, 925 silver, partly oxidized, pearls; 2009, 50 × 65 × 25 mm, 925 silver, oxidized, pearls, Binchō-tan charcoal; 2009, 60 × 70 × 40 mm, 925 silver, partly oxidized, pearls

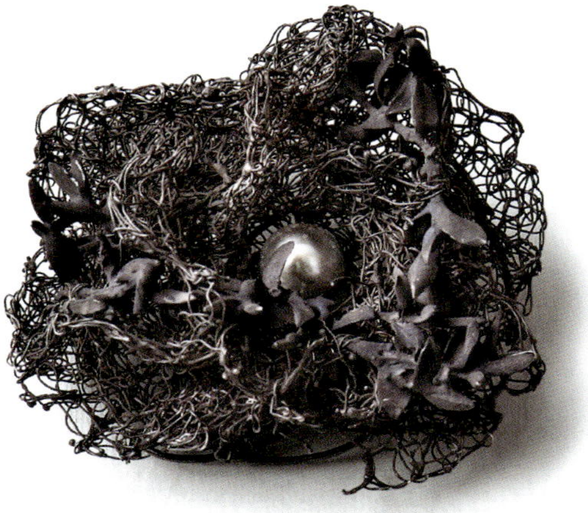

Brooch, 2008, 75 × 70 × 45 mm, 925 silver, oxidized, Tahiti pearl

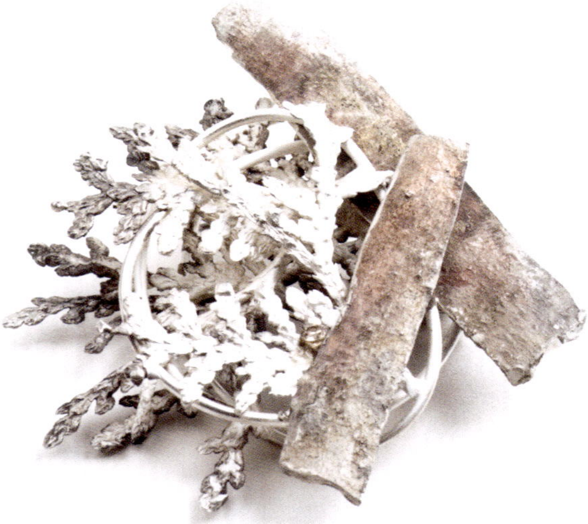

Brooch, 2009, 70 × 75 × 20 mm, 925 silver, diamond

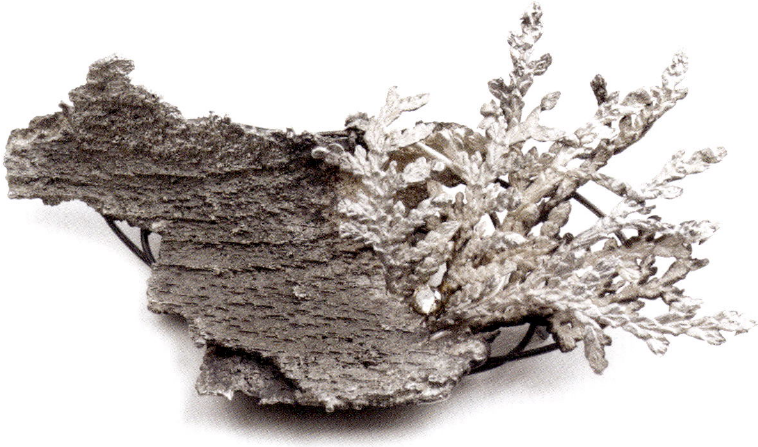

Brooch, 2009, 105 × 60 × 20 mm, 925 silver, partly oxidized, diamond

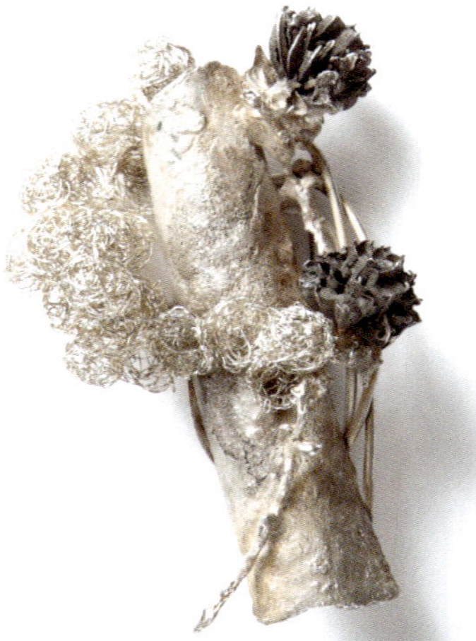

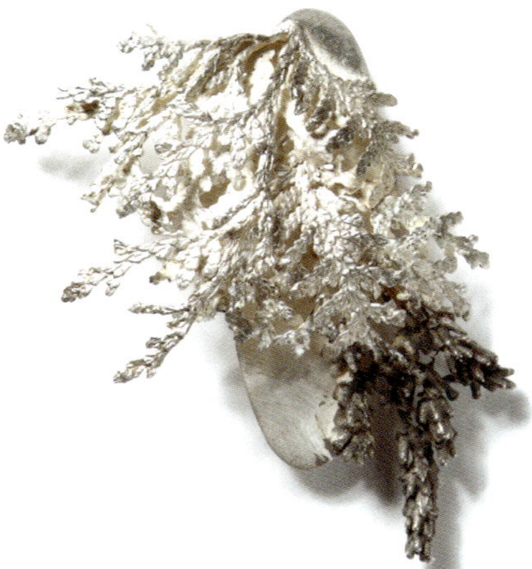

Brooches, 2010. L–R 55 × 80 × 30 mm, 80 × 95 × 30 mm, 925 silver, partly oxidized

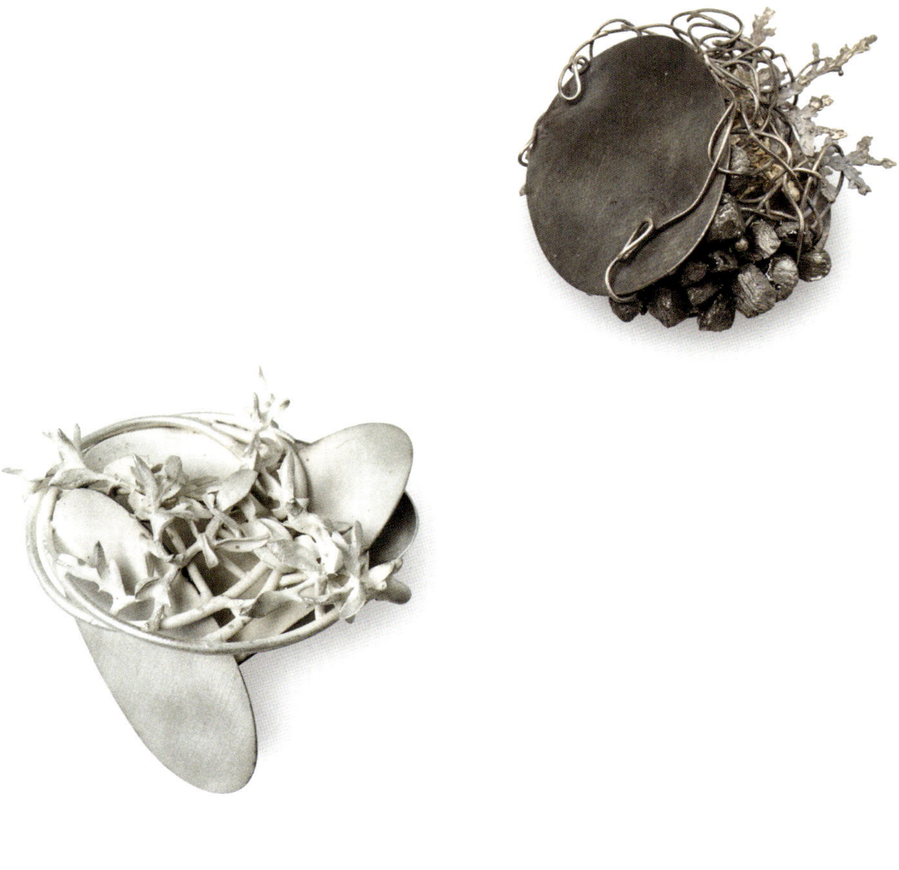

Brooches, 2008. L–R 70 × 70 × 35 mm, 925 silver, fine silver-plated; 65 × 70 × 25 mm, 925 silver, cxidized, Binchō-tan charcoal

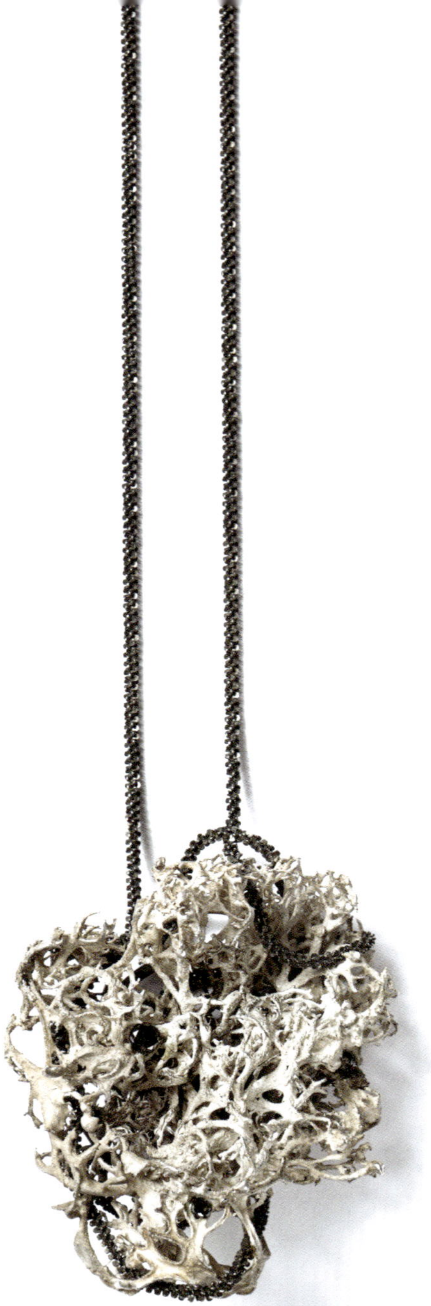

Neckpiece, 2010, 570 × 70 × 45 mm, 925 silver, partly oxidized, black diamonds

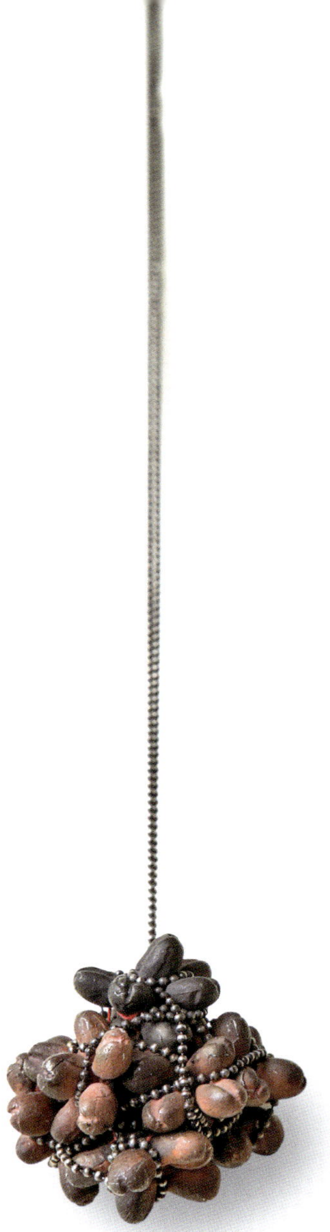

Neckpiece, 2010, 560 × 45 × 40 mm, 925 silver, partly oxidized, silk

Moonlight Shadow

JORUNN VEITEBERG

Mari Ishikawa sent me a photo. It has clearly been taken in the dark; only the middle section is lit up. We are out in nature. Green ferns stretch outwards from clefts in the rock face, a reminder to us of just how hardy certain plants are. Ferns often seek out places where there are no other plants. They can survive on rock surfaces and where there is shade. Perhaps it is these properties that appeal to Mari Ishikawa. For a number of years, the fern has been a key motif in the series of jewellery she has called *Moonlight Shadow*. The fern-form can twine into a ring or be one of several elements in brooches and necklaces. But apart from symbolising hardiness and survival, the fern is also a plant with great aesthetic qualities. Its many serrations form an organic, ornamental structure that appeals to our need for beauty.

Many people associate jewellery with celebrations. Just as we use flowers and plants to mark festive occasions and for decorative purposes, many people use jewellery to adorn themselves. To use plants as a motif in jewellery is thus logical. Ishikawa's use, however, does not correspond to our expectations, for her nature reference breaks with the conventional ideas of what is festive. In the *Moonlight Shadow* series she uses, among other things, casts from empty seed capsules, pieces of bark, and lichen. They often form a chaotic composition – seen with Western eyes, at any rate. She often includes a string of pearls that represent more conventional ideas of beauty and jewellery. The combination challenges us to reflect on what beauty is and can be. The tension between the chaotic and the cultivated is also a recurrent feature of the series.

The richness of colour found in nature is not something Ishikawa celebrates. Even though colours are important to her, she is highly economical with them. A common theme has recurred in her work, symbolising her link to her native country, Japan. But in the series *Moonlight Shadow* it is nature and the landscape as experienced in the pale light of the moon that is the theme. In this light, the world is grey. Normally, grey is considered to be a neutral colour that occupies a position between the extremities of black and white. In the West, this neutrality has given rise to two different interpretations. Grey can symbolise both the elegant and sophisticated as well as the insipid and sad. In Japan, on the other hand, grey has a much richer palette, and there are at least a hundred words for this colour.

As the title indicates, the moon is a keyword for this series. Just as the sun is connected with life, the moon is connected with death. And just as darkness and moonlight creates mystery in her photographs, there is a melancholy ambience to this jewellery. The grey-white colour scale that makes the forms resemble frozen nature are important in creating this mood, but this choice also serves to detach the motives from the realism opened up by the casting technique. Ishikawa's aim is not to give a true depiction of what the world looks like but to open up our minds to other realities. As she herself formulates it, 'I try to freeze the plants' beauty and stop the process of fading by keeping their essence and their memories.' In the shadow landscape of the moon the imagination is given a freer rein. The forms of nature are transformed and can represent something completely different from what they were before. And we suspect that the nature we meet in this jewellery is perhaps first and foremost emotional in character.

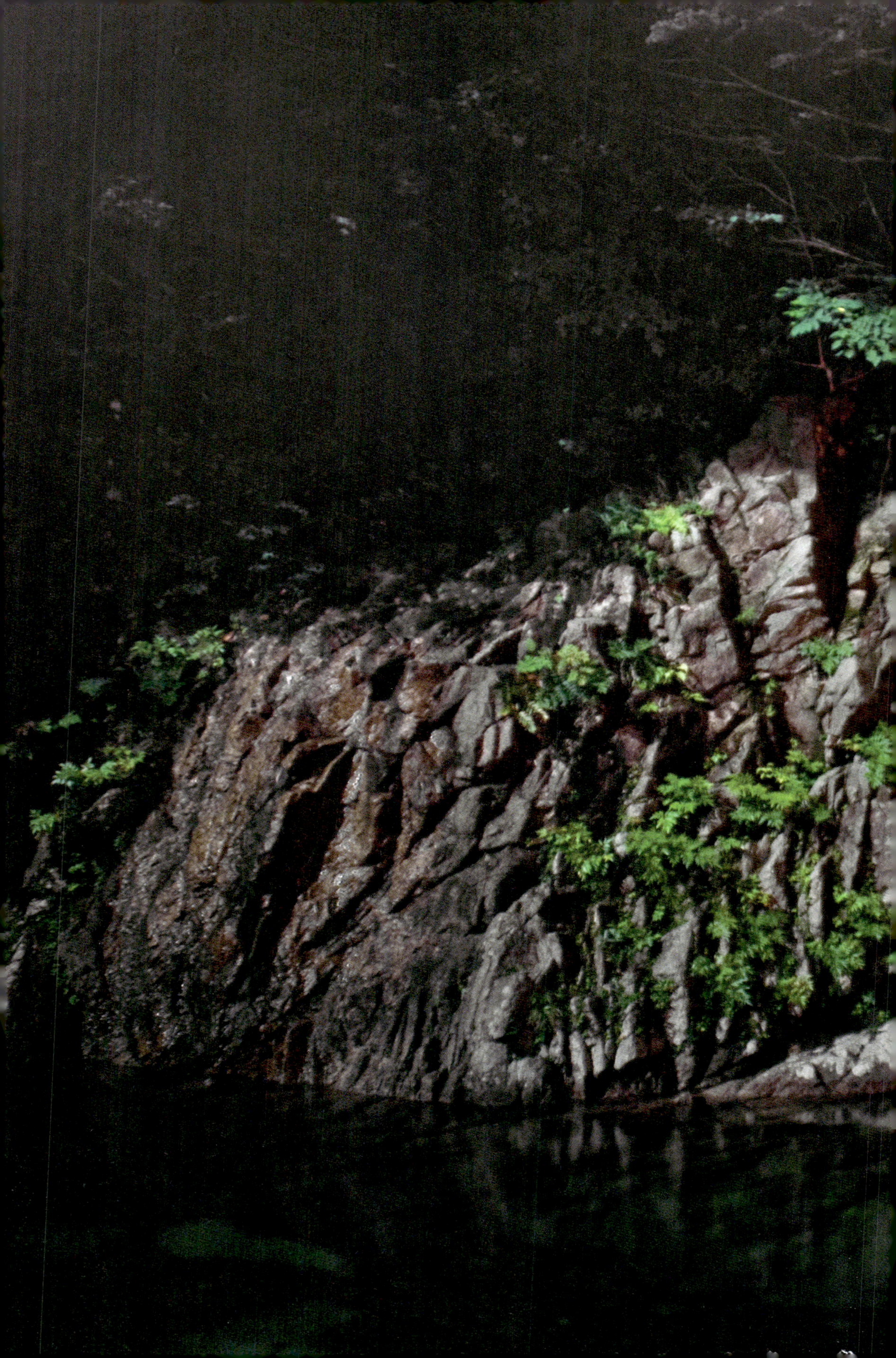

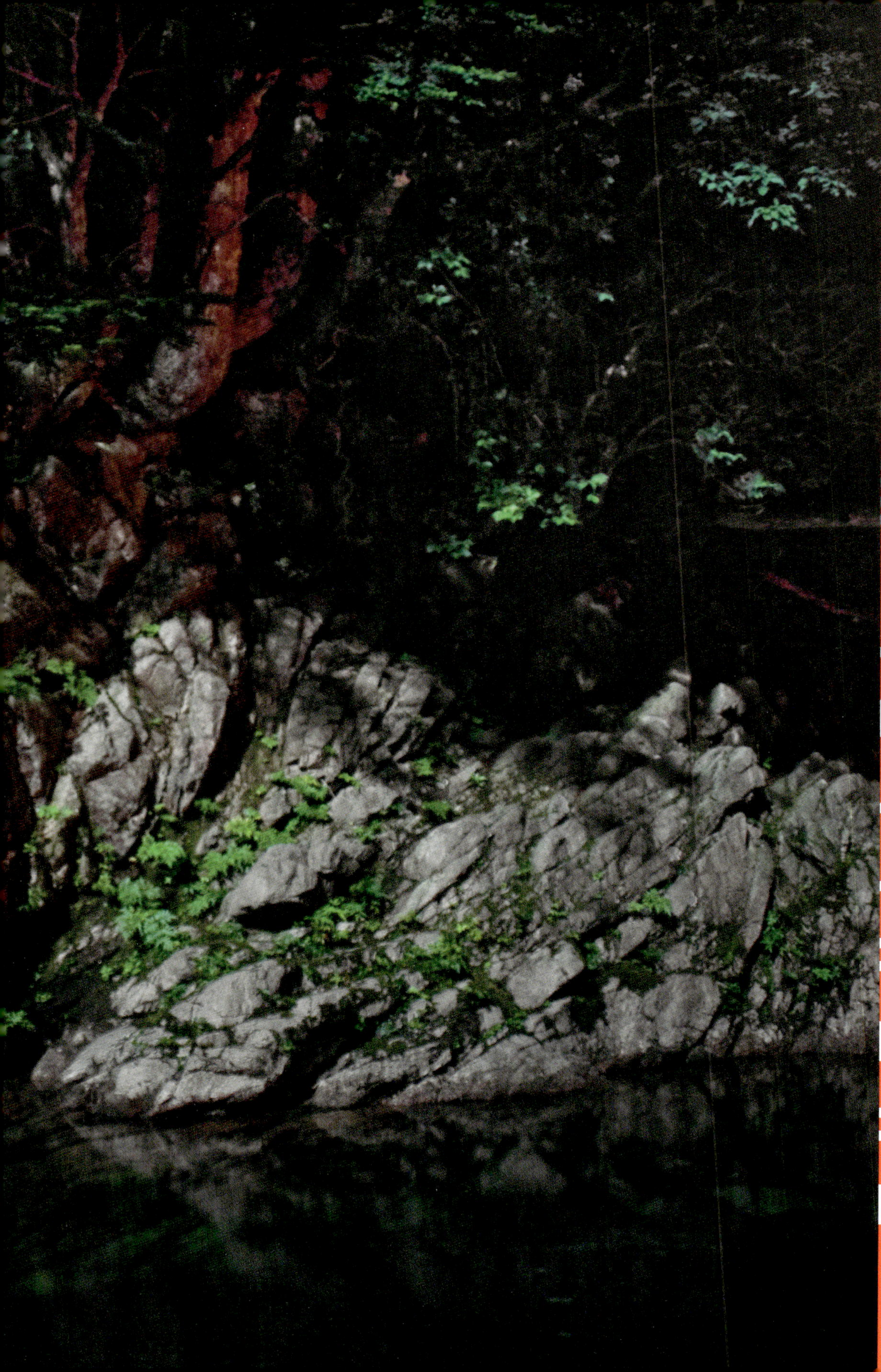

HANGING GARDEN

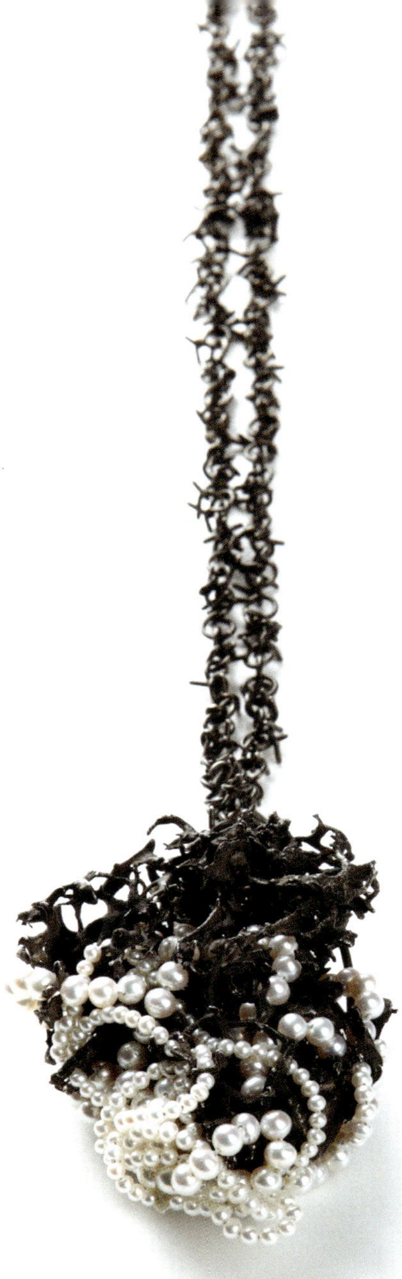

Neckpiece, 2012, 500 × 60 × 40 mm, 925 silver, oxidized, pearls

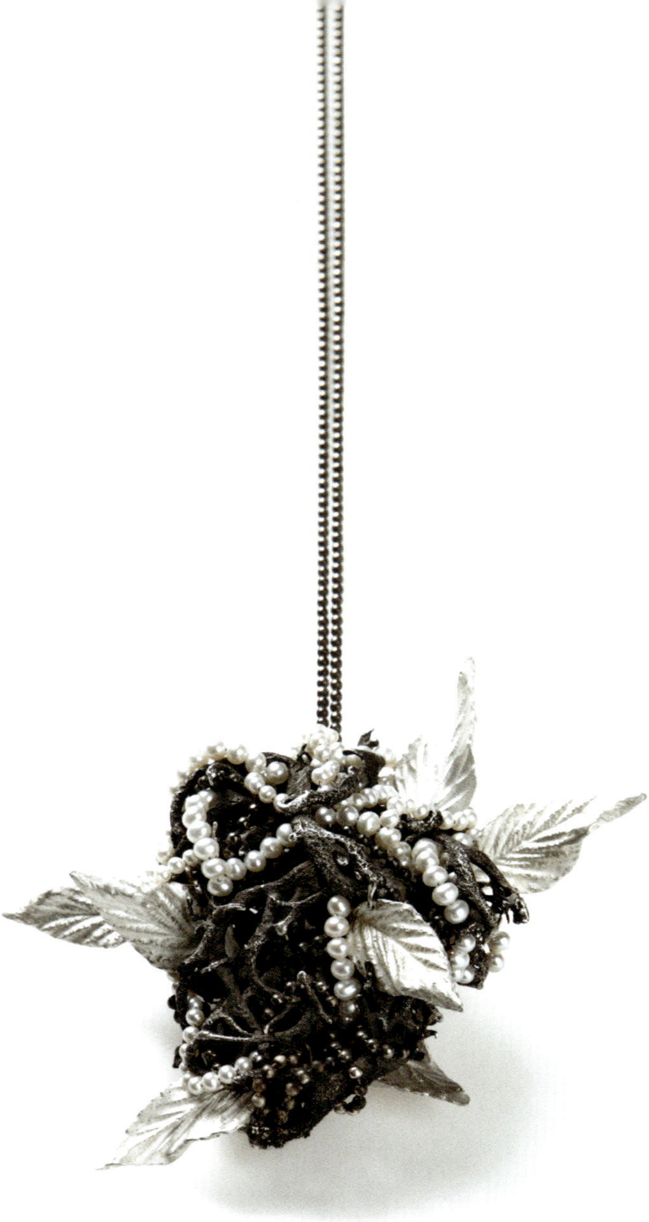

Neckpiece, 2011, 560 × 95 × 40 mm, 925 silver, partly oxidized, pearls

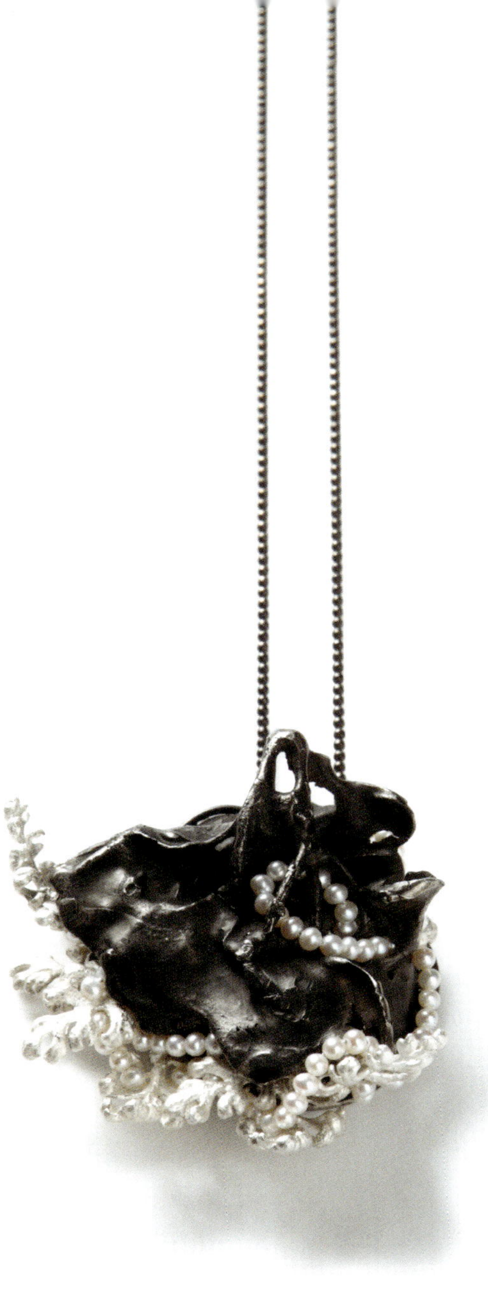

Neckpiece, 2011, 560 × 95 × 35 mm, 925 silver, oxidized, pearls

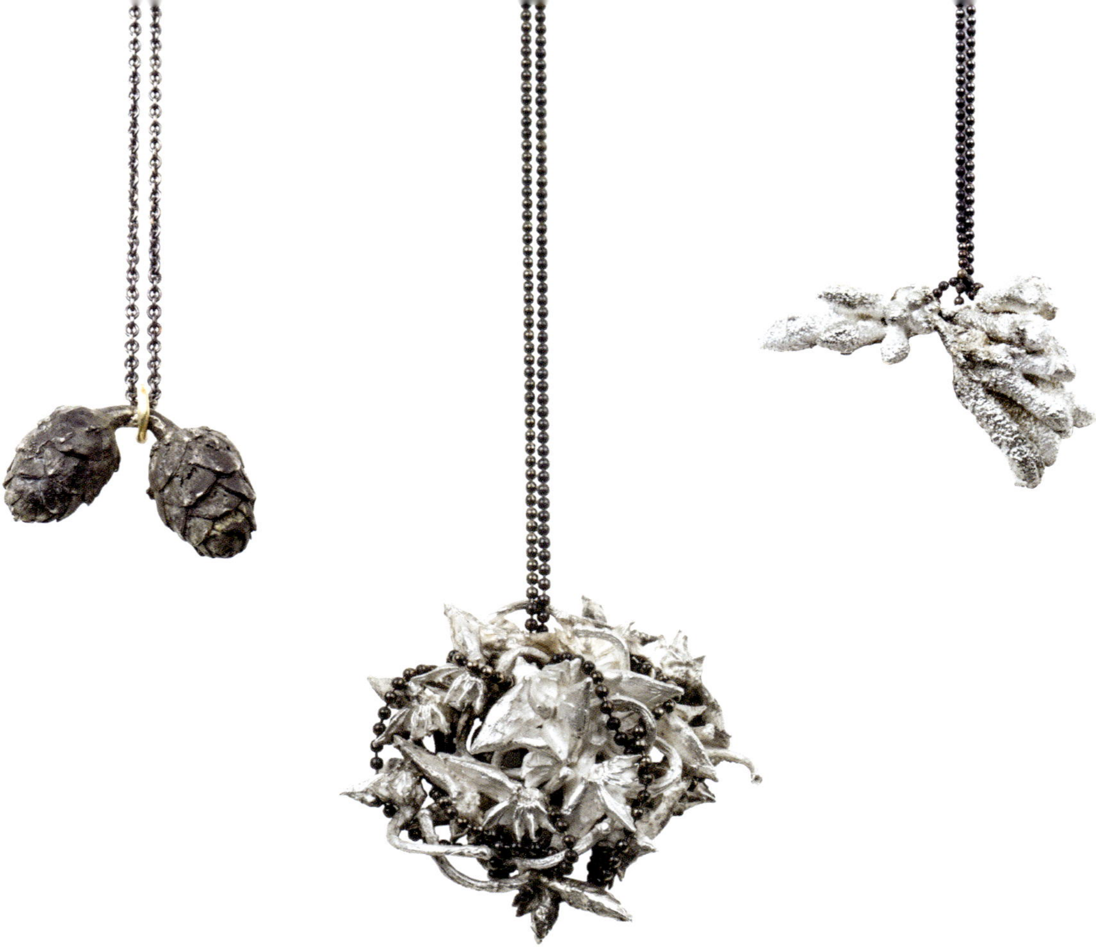

Pendants, 2010, L–R 510 × 40 × 15 mm, 750 gold, 925 silver, oxidized; 570 × 60 × 35 mm, 925 silver, partly oxidized; 530 × 40 × 20 mm, 925 silver, partly oxidized
Page 85: Pendants, 2010, L–R 2010, 520 × 30 × 25 mm, 925 silver, oxidized; 2009, 570 × 75 × 20 mm, 925 silver, partly oxidized; 530 × 40 × 35 mm, 925 silver, partly oxidized

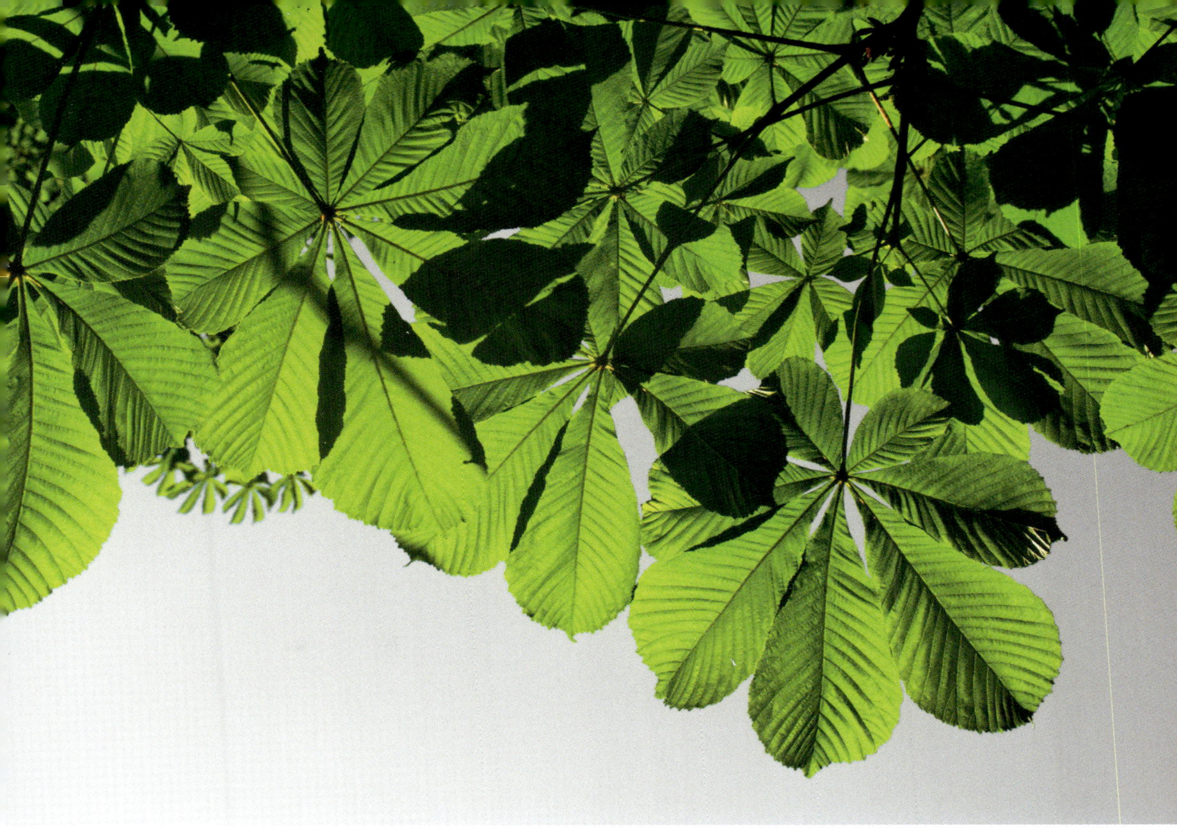

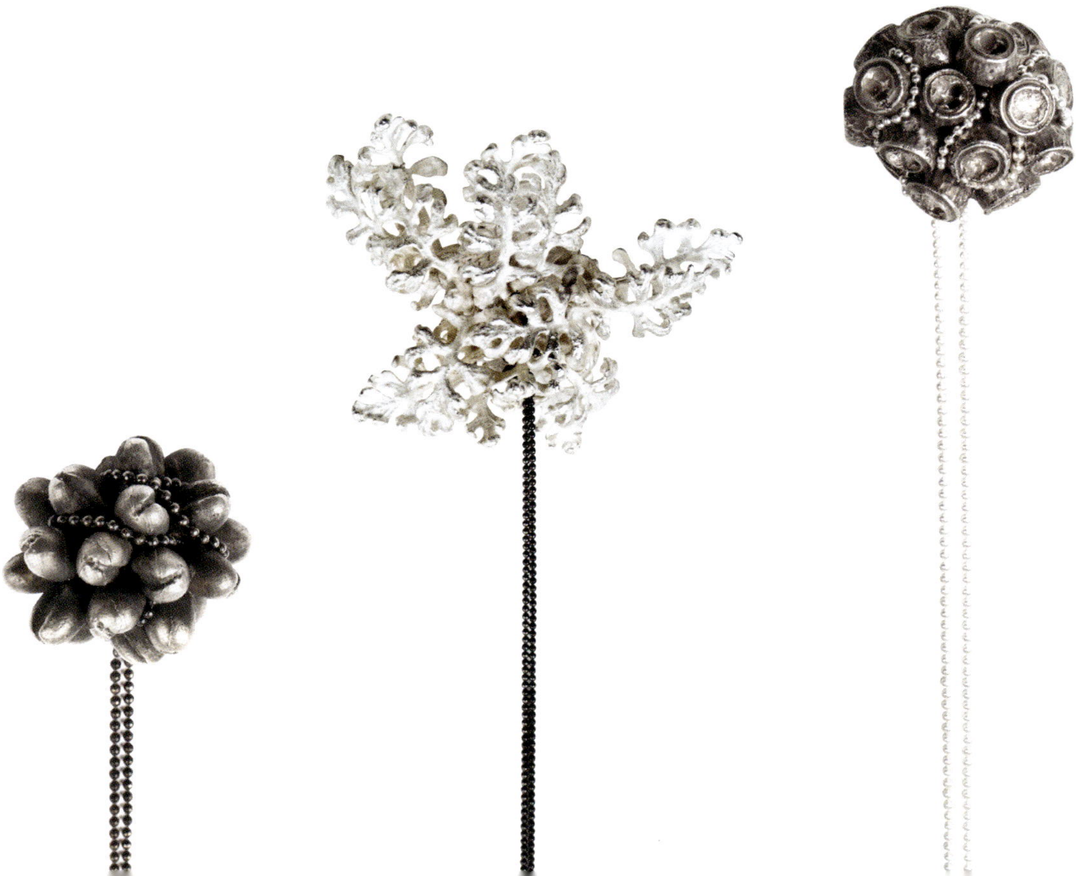

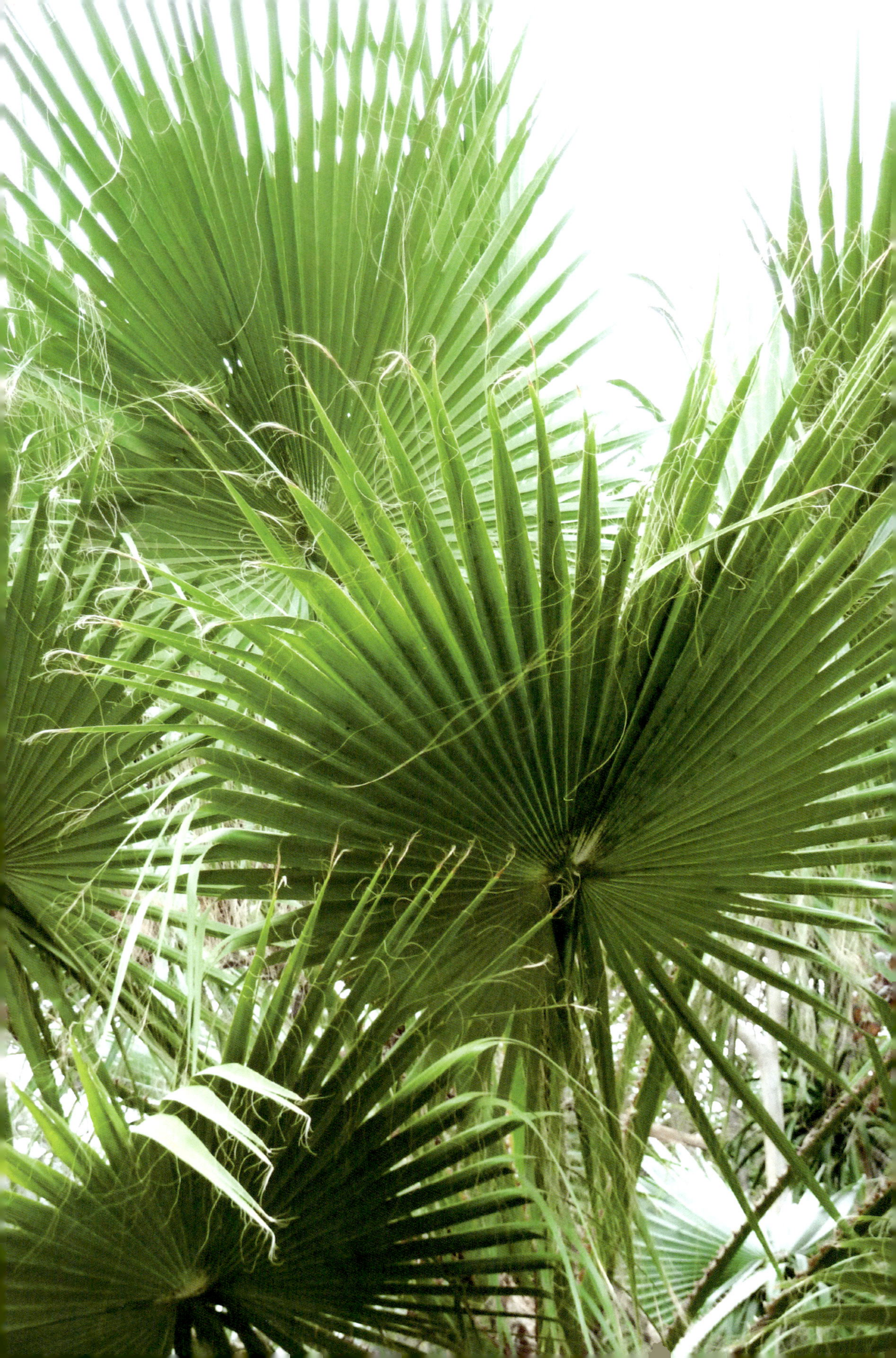

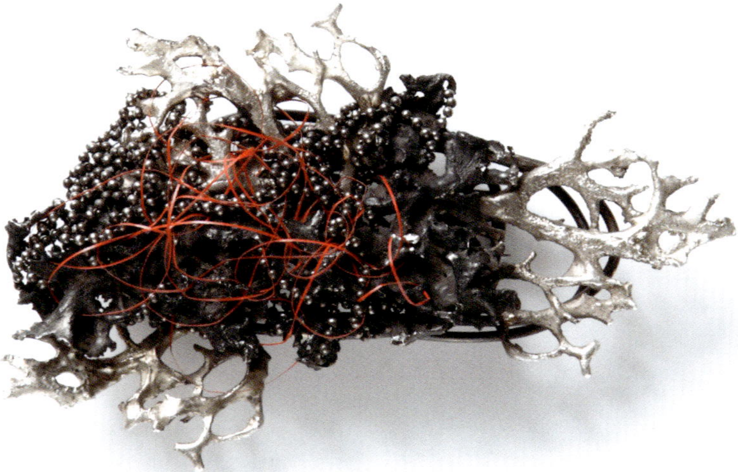

Brooch, 2012, 90 × 60 × 25 mm, 925 silver, partly oxidized, Japanese lacquer tape

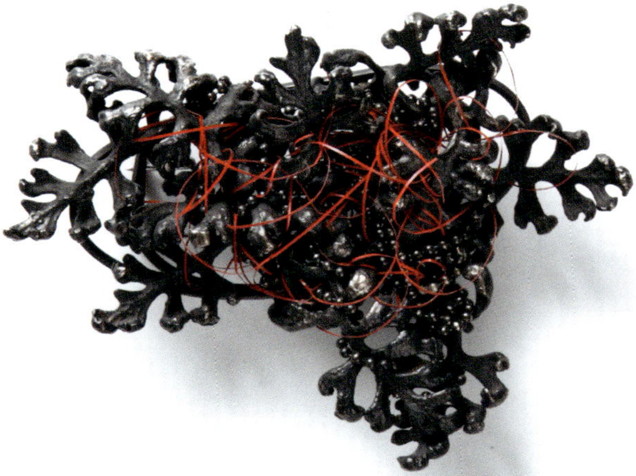

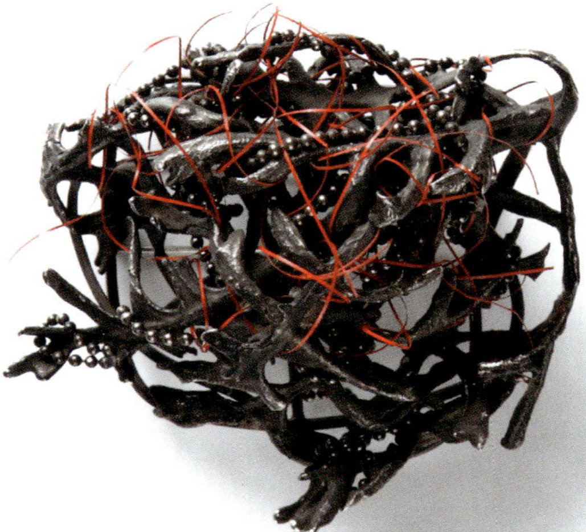

Brooches, 2012, T–B 100 × 55 × 30 mm, 65 × 55 × 40 mm, 925 silver, oxidized, Japanese lacquer tape

PARALLEL WORLD

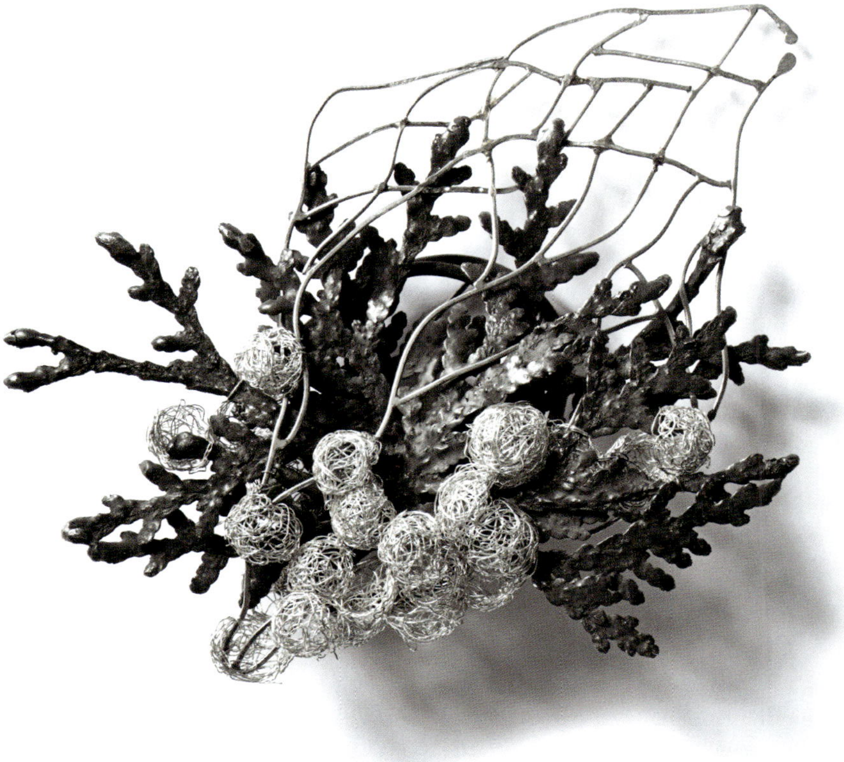

Brooch, 2011, 125 × 95 × 35 mm, 925 silver, partly oxidized

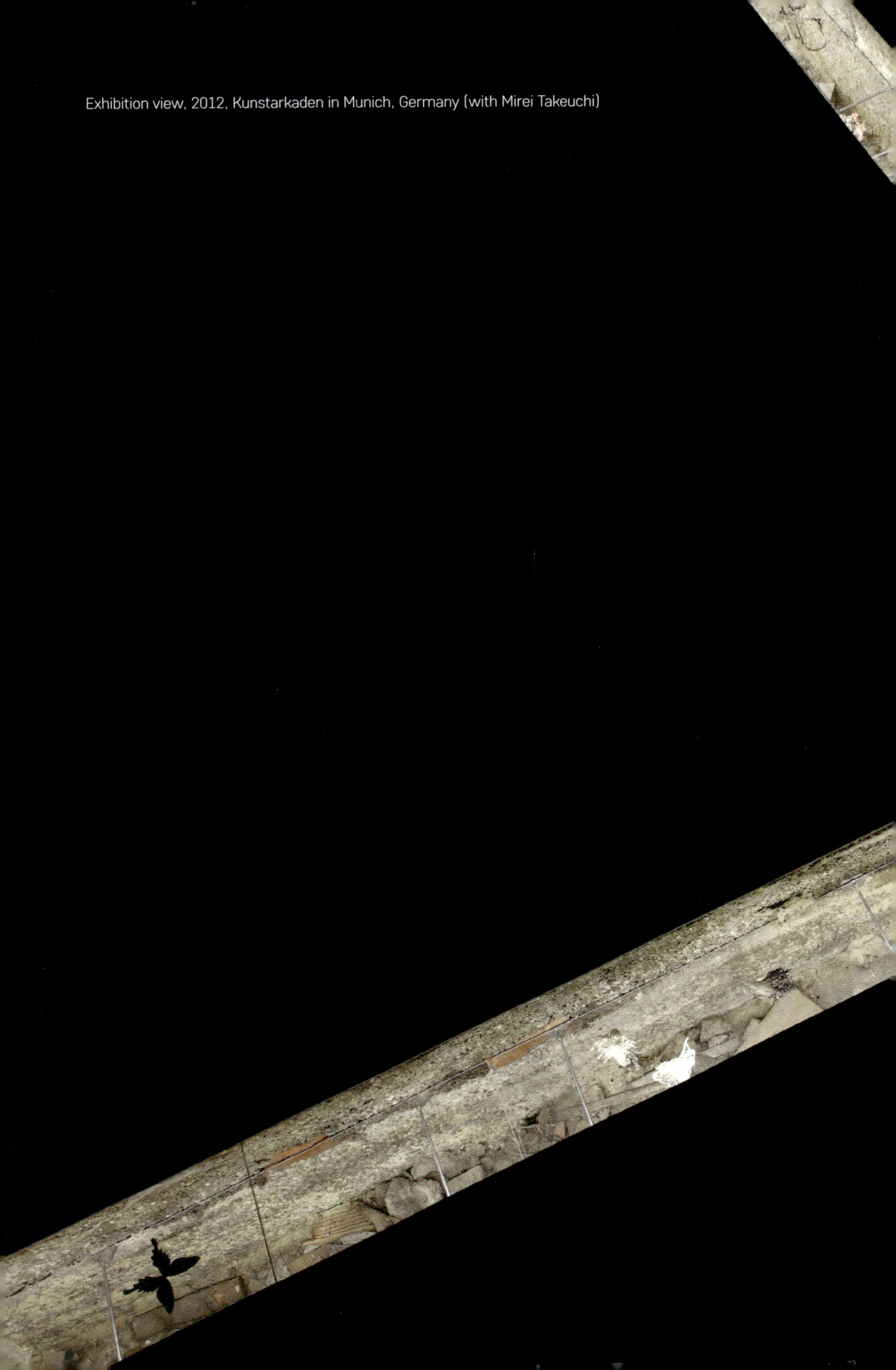

Exhibition view, 2012, Kunstarkaden in Munich, Germany (with Mirei Takeuchi)

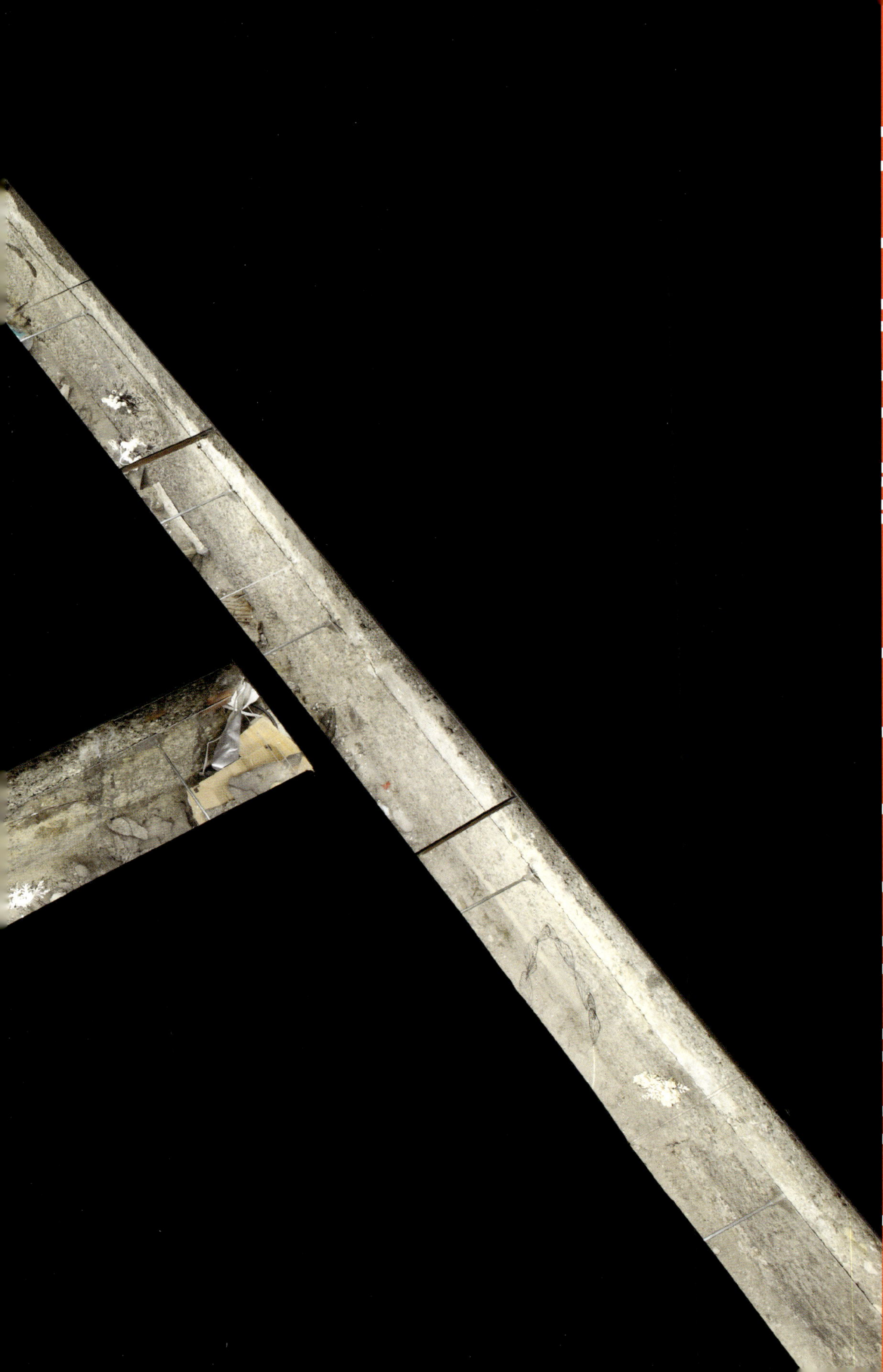

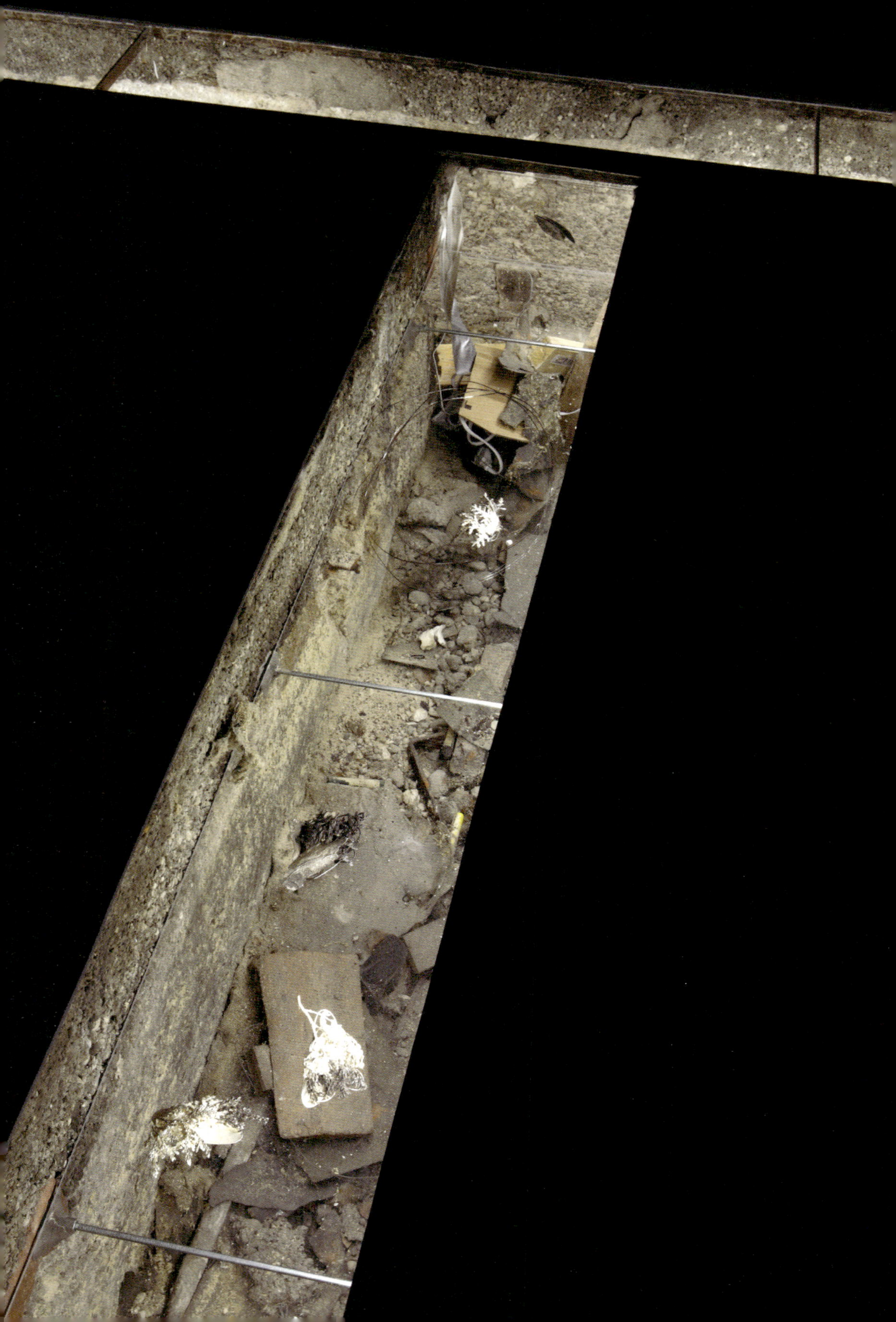

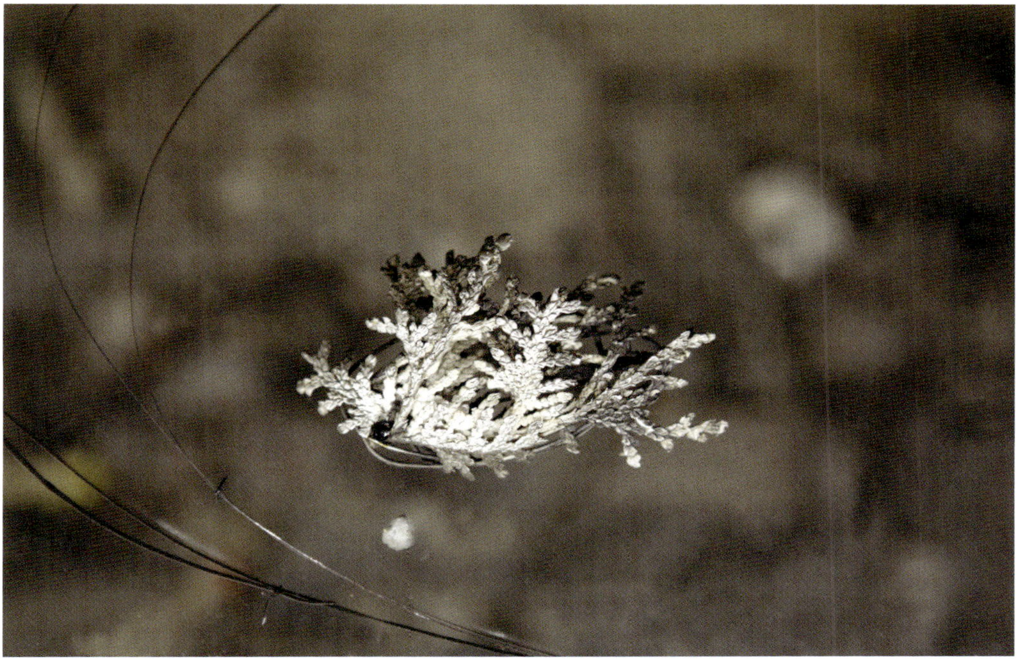

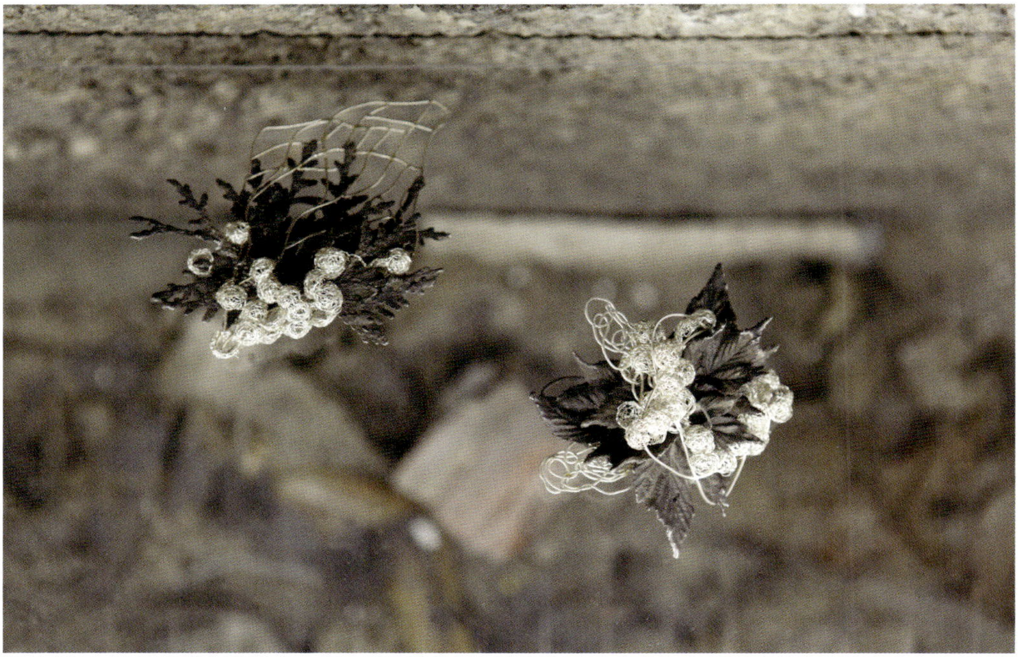

Exhibition views, 2012, Kunstarkaden in Munich, Germany (with Mirei Takeuchi)

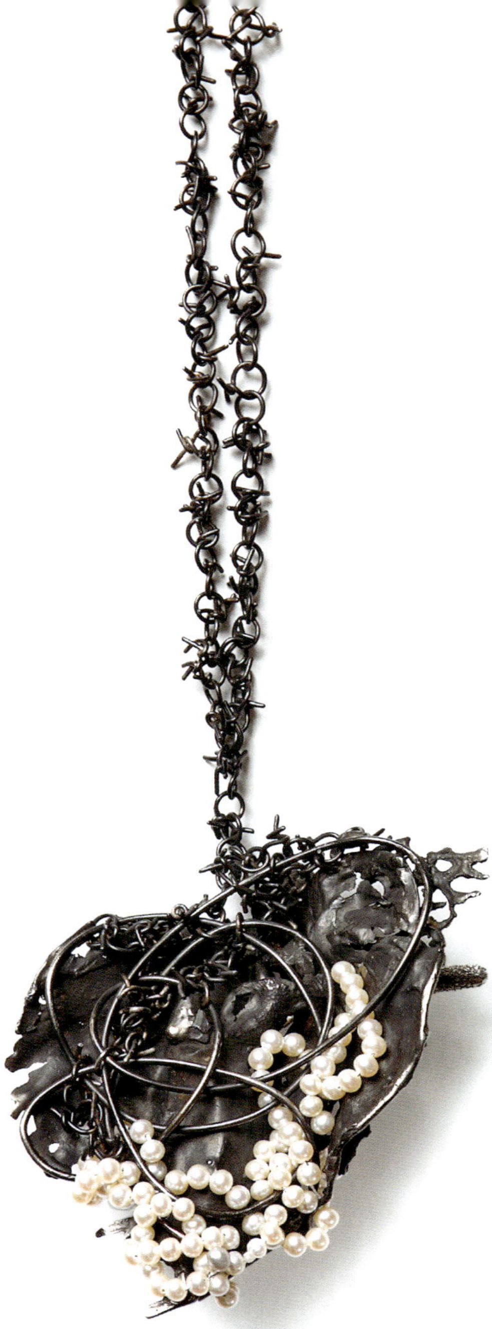

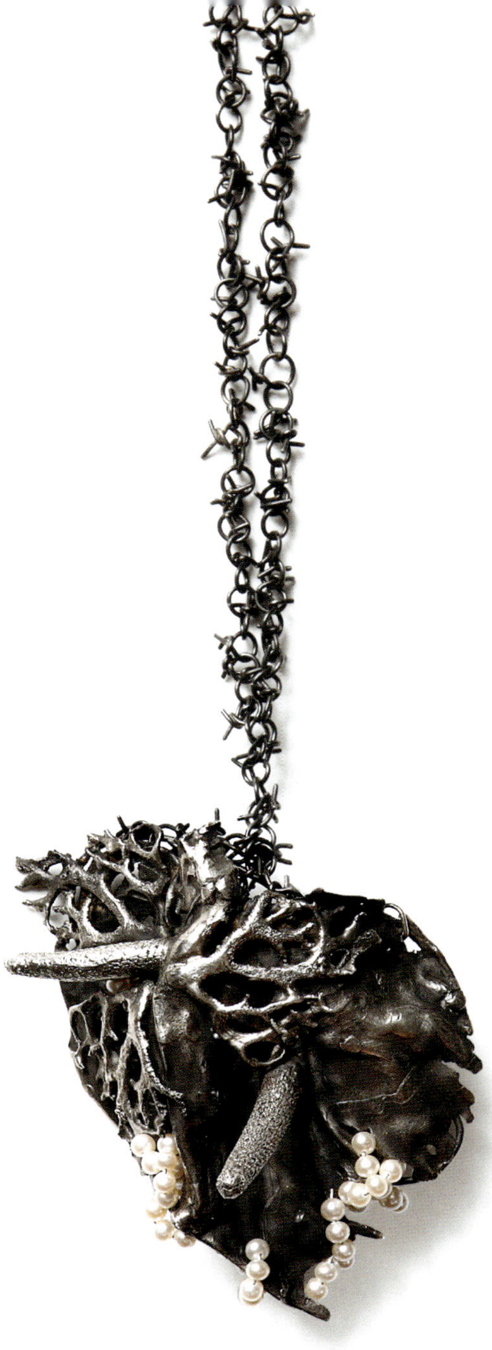

Neckpiece (front and back view), 2012, 550 × 85 × 50 mm, 925 silver, oxidized, pearls

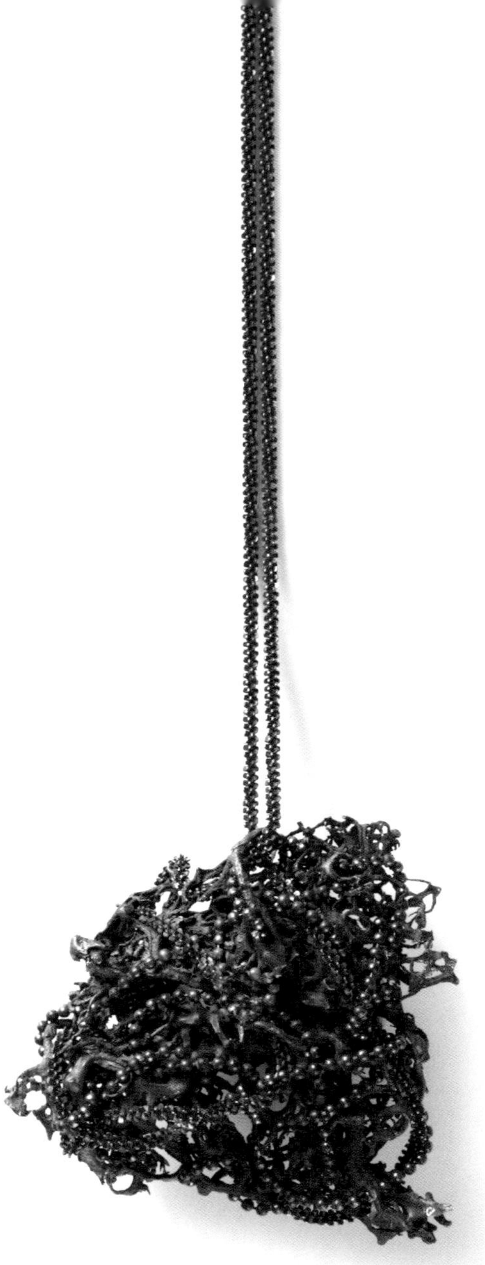

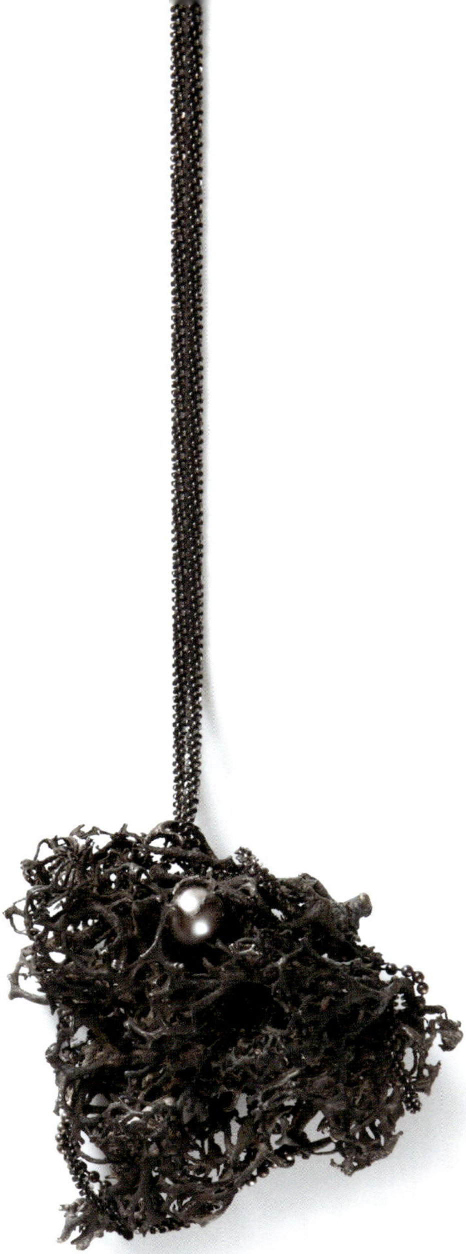

Neckpiece (front and back view), 2012, 500 × 70 × 40 mm, 925 silver, oxidized, Tahiti pearls

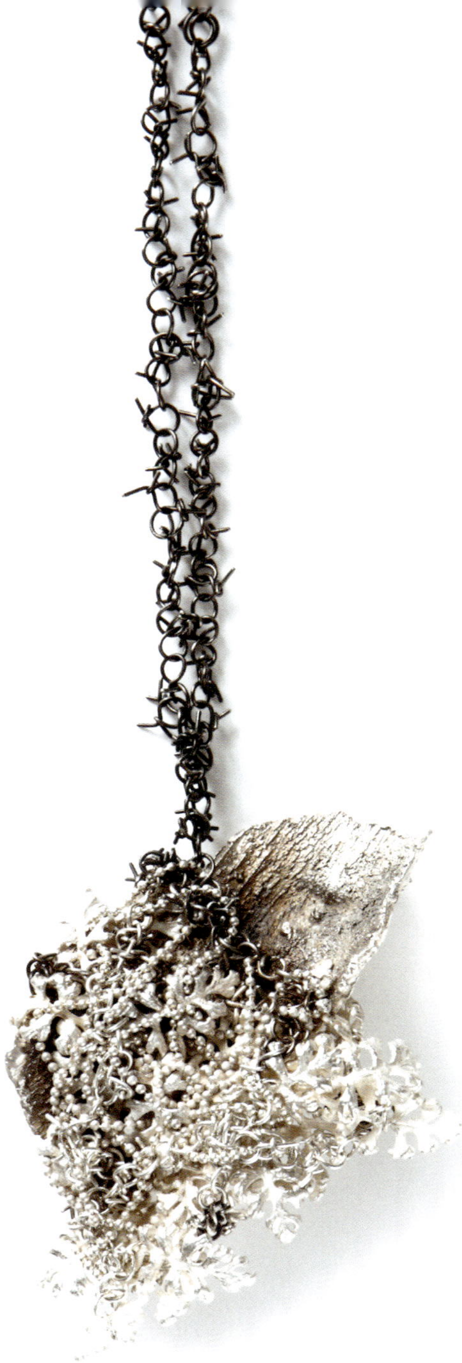

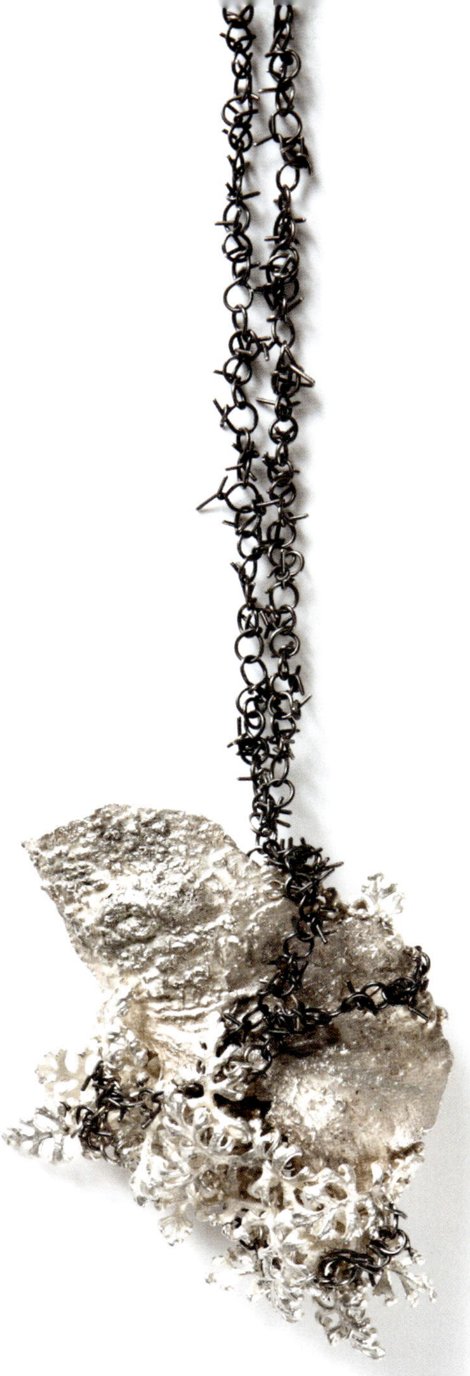

Neckpiece (front and back view), 2012, 560 × 90 × 40 mm, 925 silver, partly oxidized, pearls

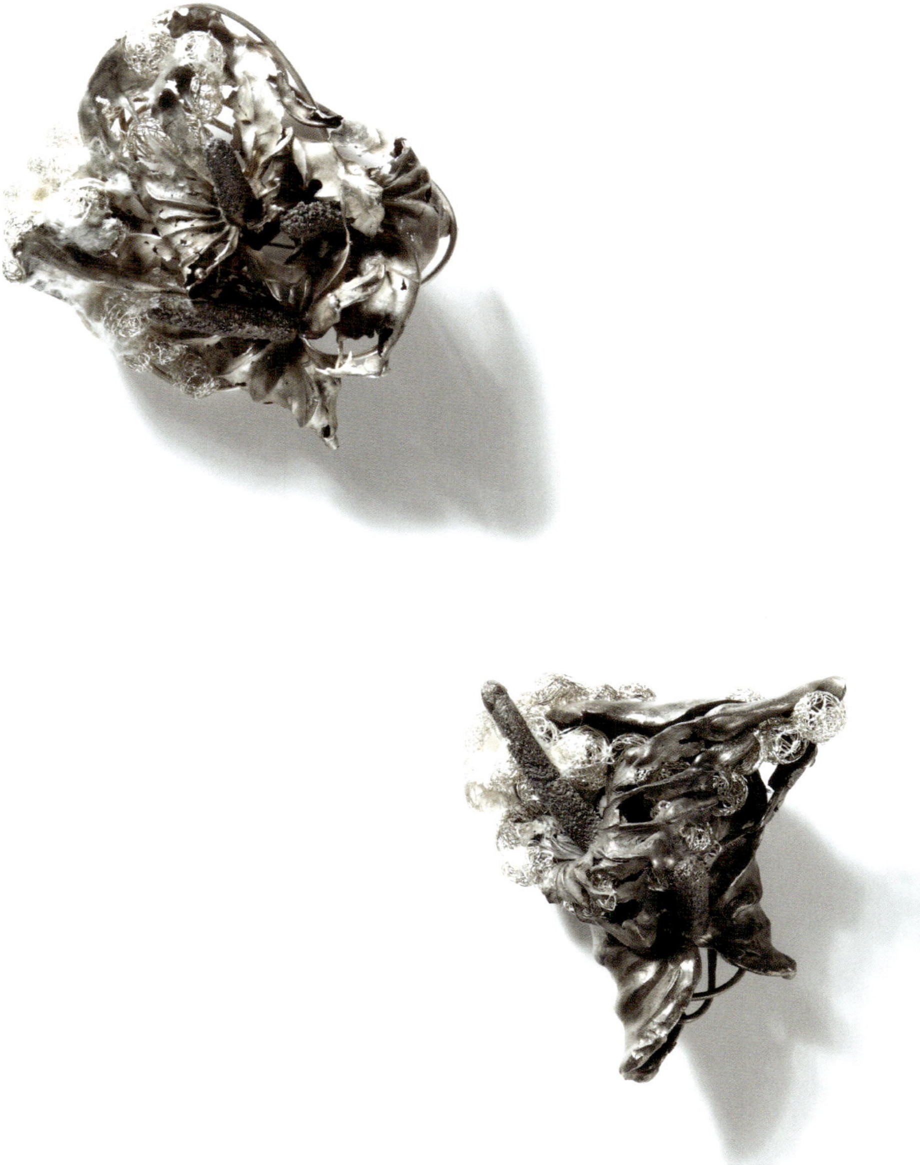

Brooches, 2011, L–R 90 × 85 × 45 mm, 75 × 85 × 50 mm, 925 silver, partly oxidized, Japanese Kozo paper

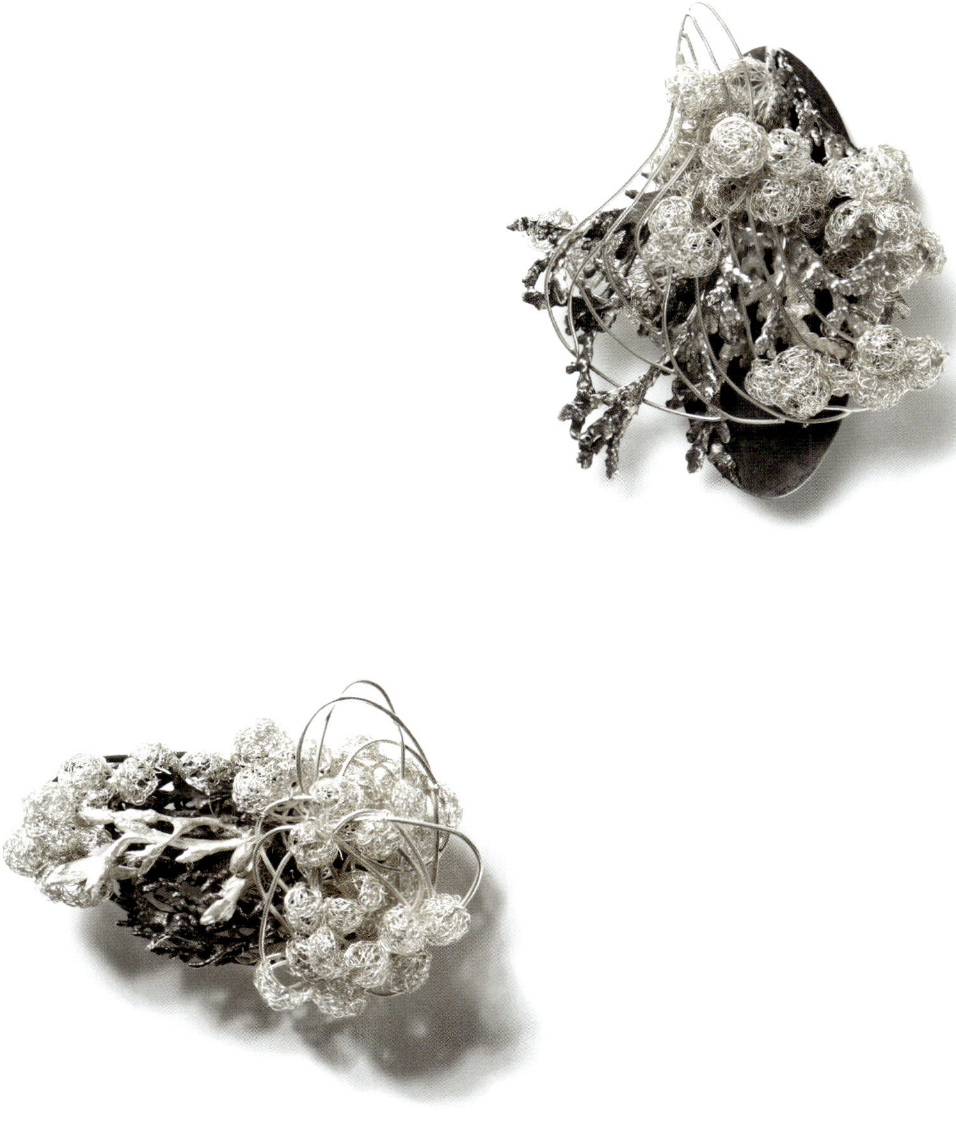

Brooches, 2011, L–R 90 × 70 × 30 mm, 80 × 100 × 30 mm, 925 silver, partly oxidized

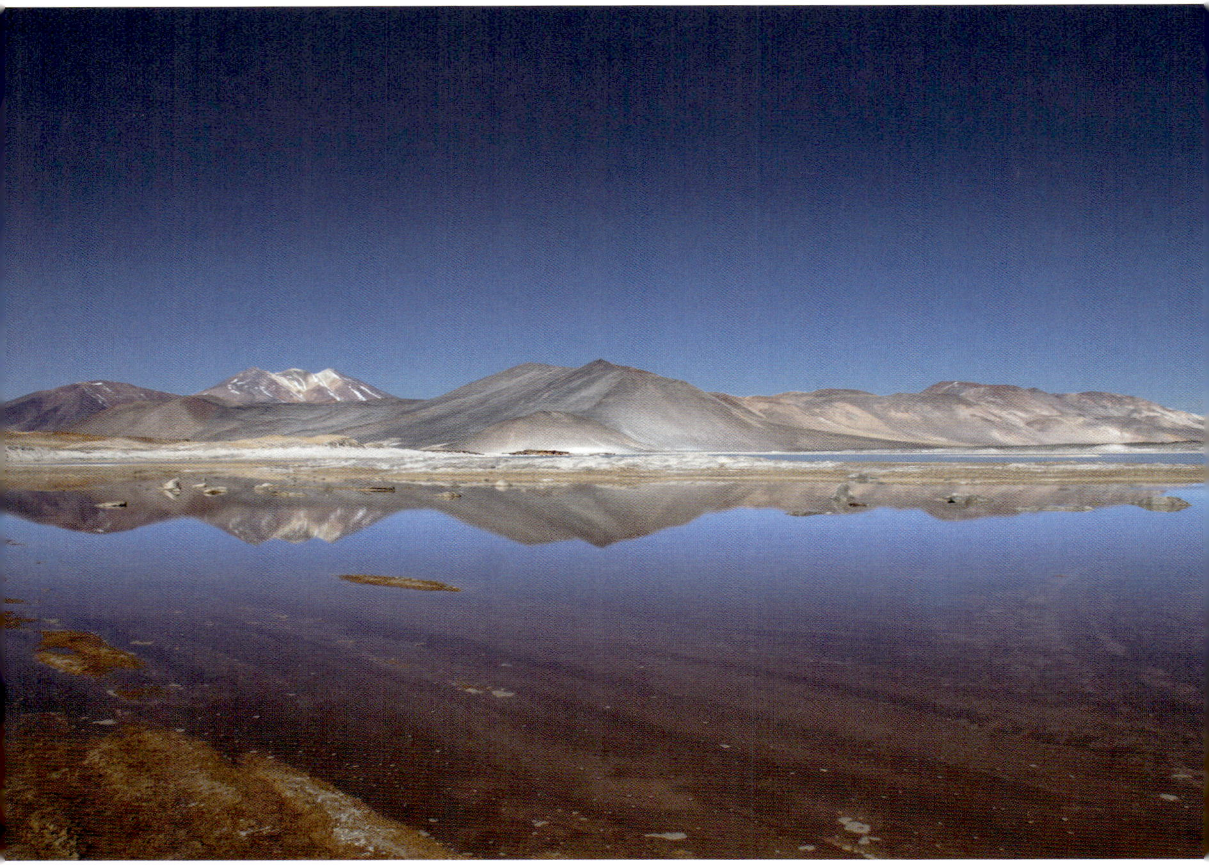

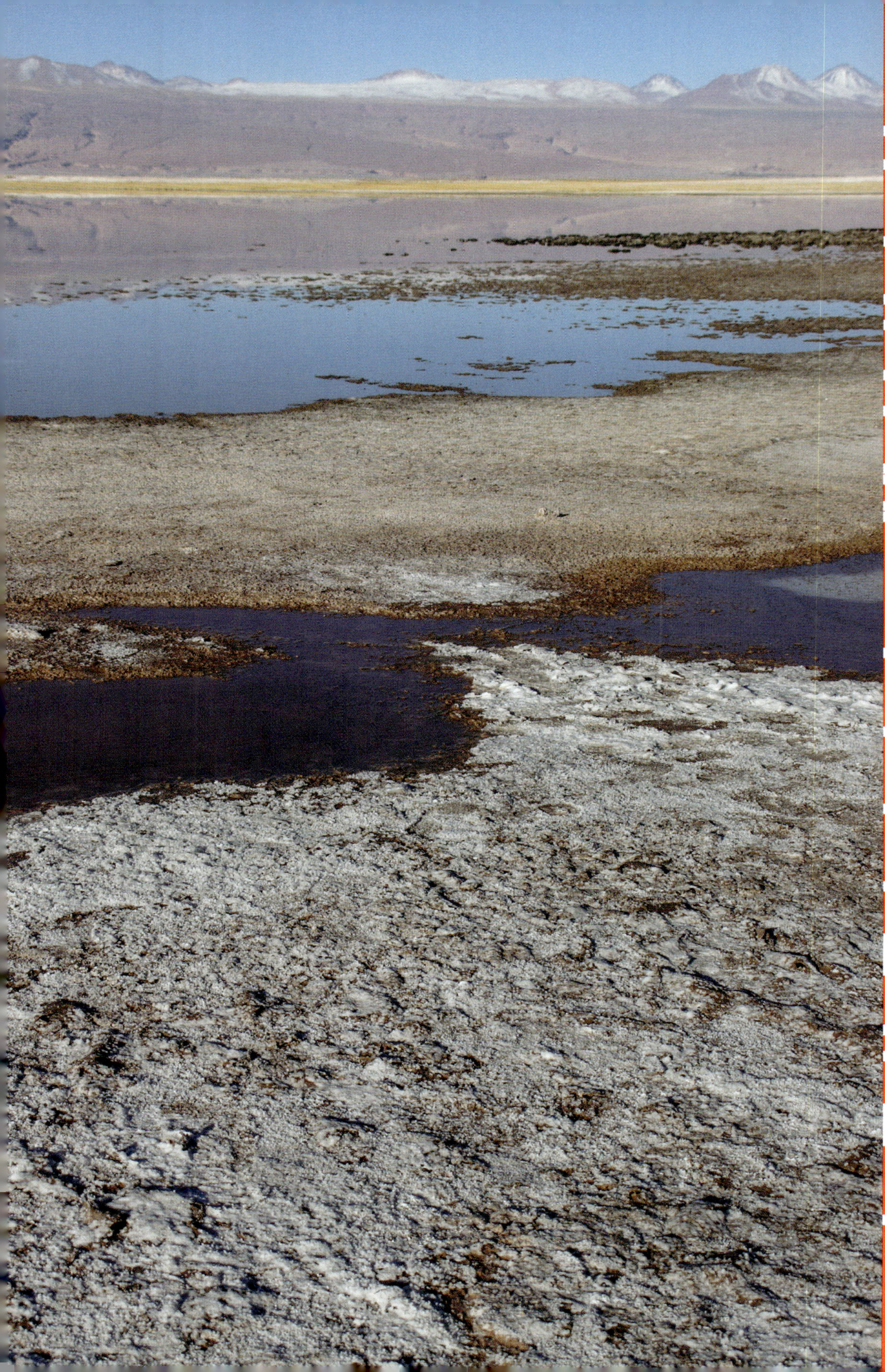

LANDSCAPE

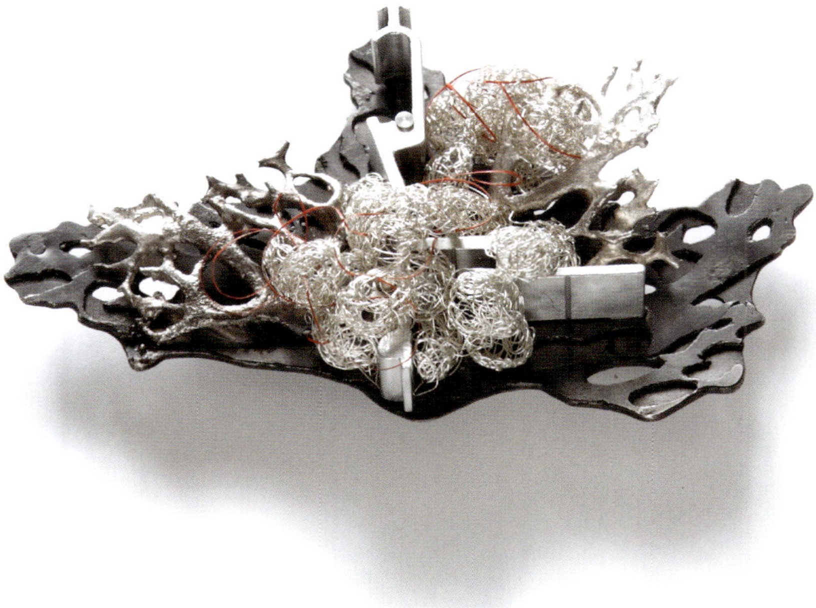

Brooch, 2012, 105 × 65 × 25 mm, 925 silver, partly oxidized, aluminium, Japanese lacquer tape

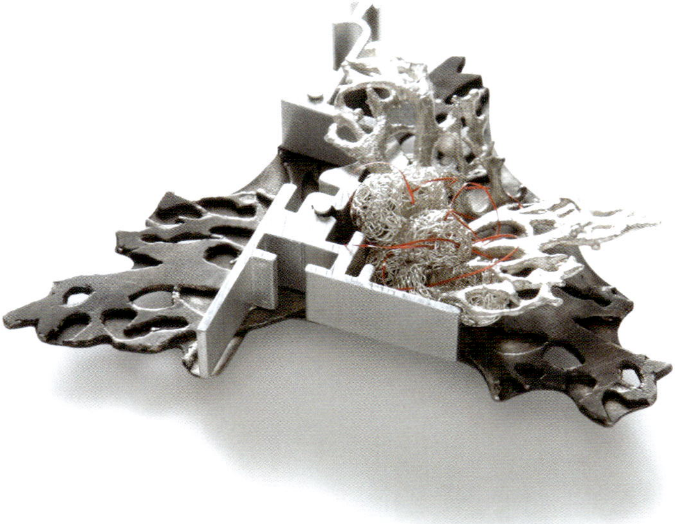

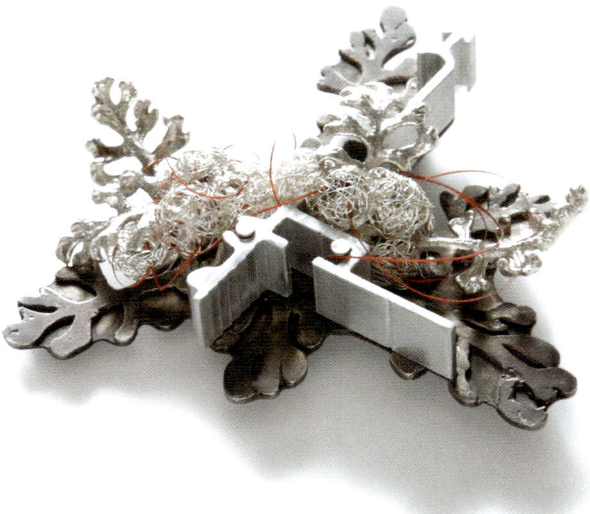

Brooches, 2012, T–B 90 × 75 × 20 mm, 90 × 80 × 30 mm, 925 silver, partly oxidized, aluminium, Japanese lacquer tape

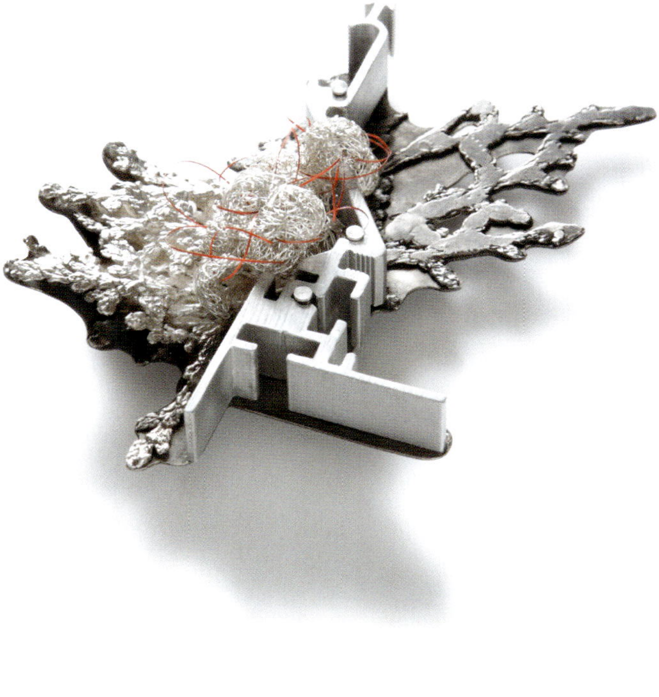

Brooch, 2012, 80 × 100 × 30 mm, 925 silver, partly oxidized, aluminium, Japanese lacquer tape

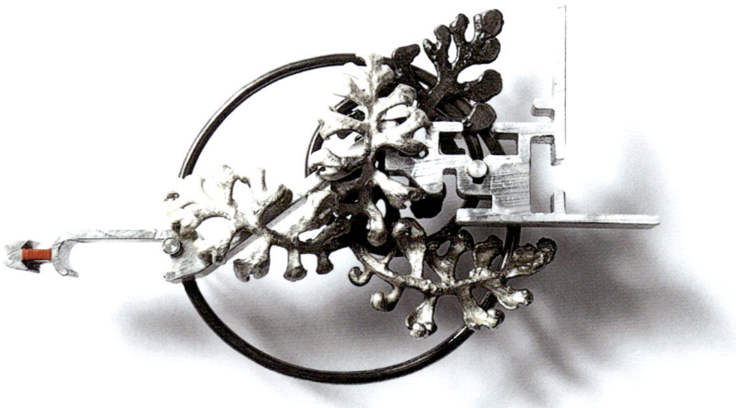

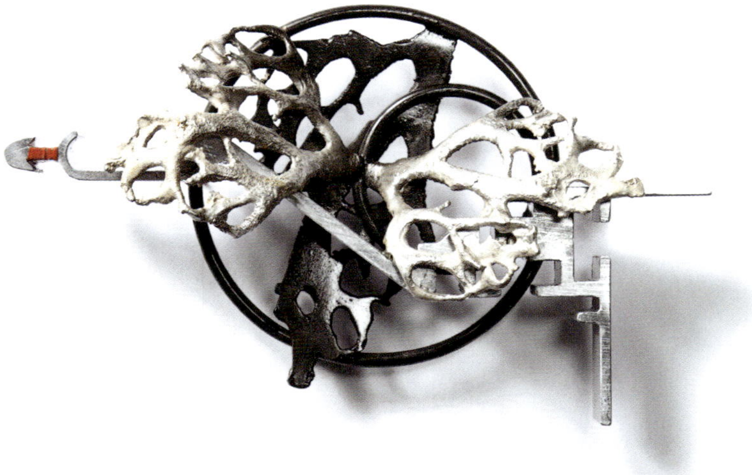

Brooches, 2013, T–B 90 × 55 × 25 mm, 90 × 55 × 30 mm, 925 silver, partly oxidized, aluminium, Japanese lacquer tape

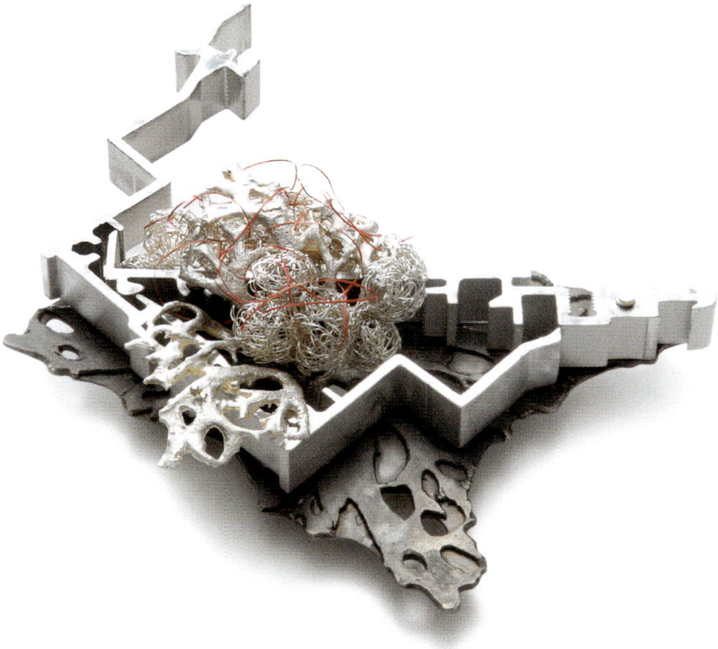

Brooch, 2013, 110 × 110 × 25 mm, 925 silver, partly oxidized, aluminium, Japanese lacquer tape

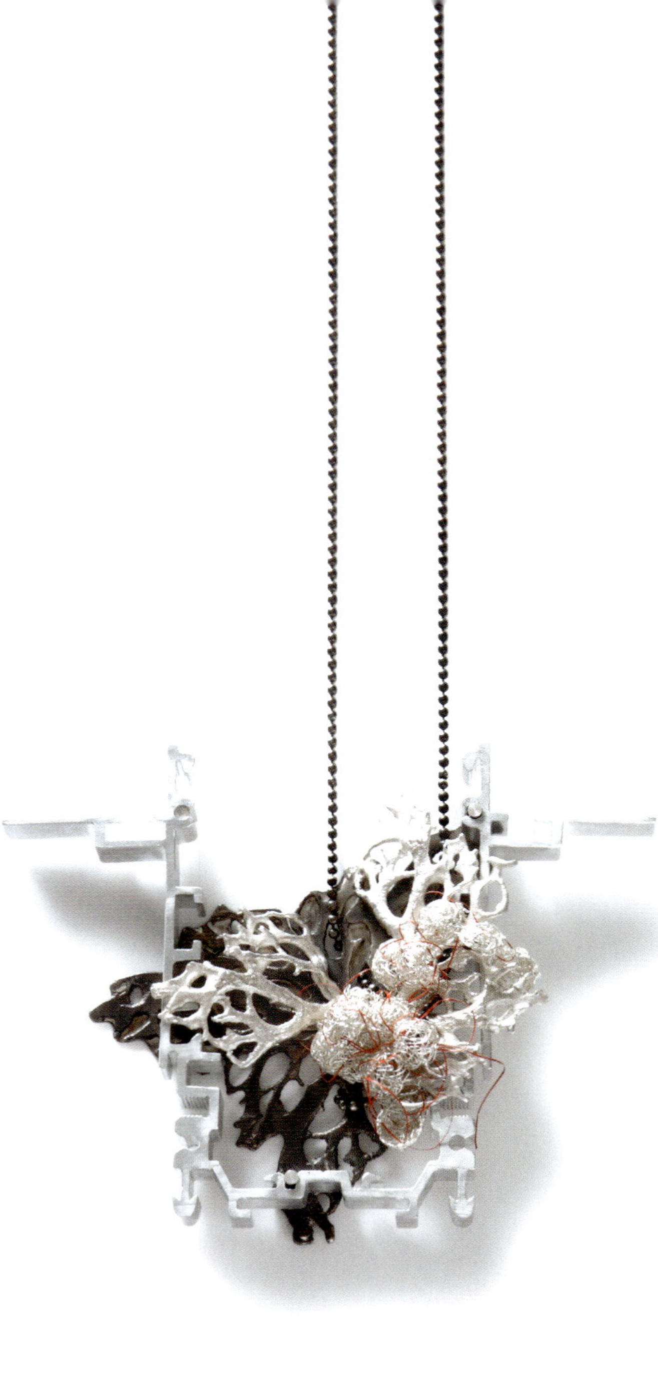

Neckpiece, 2012, 520 × 120 × 20 mm, 925 silver, partly oxidized, aluminium, Japanese lacquer tape

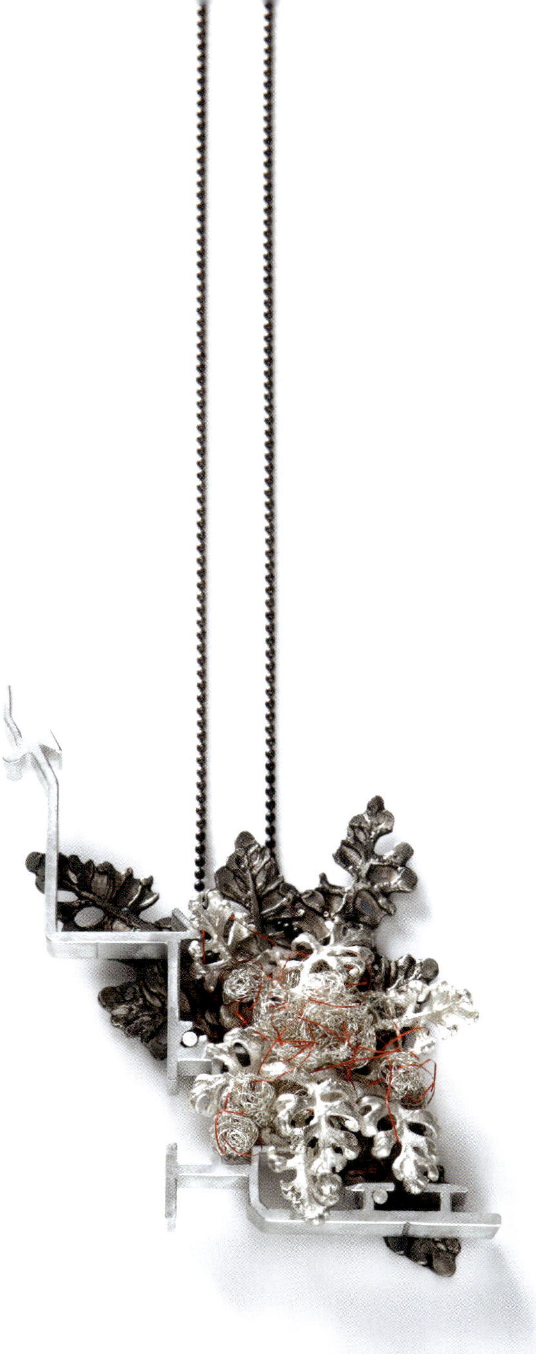

Neckpiece, 2012, 540 × 90 × 25 mm, 925 silver, partly oxidized, aluminium, Japanese lacquer tape

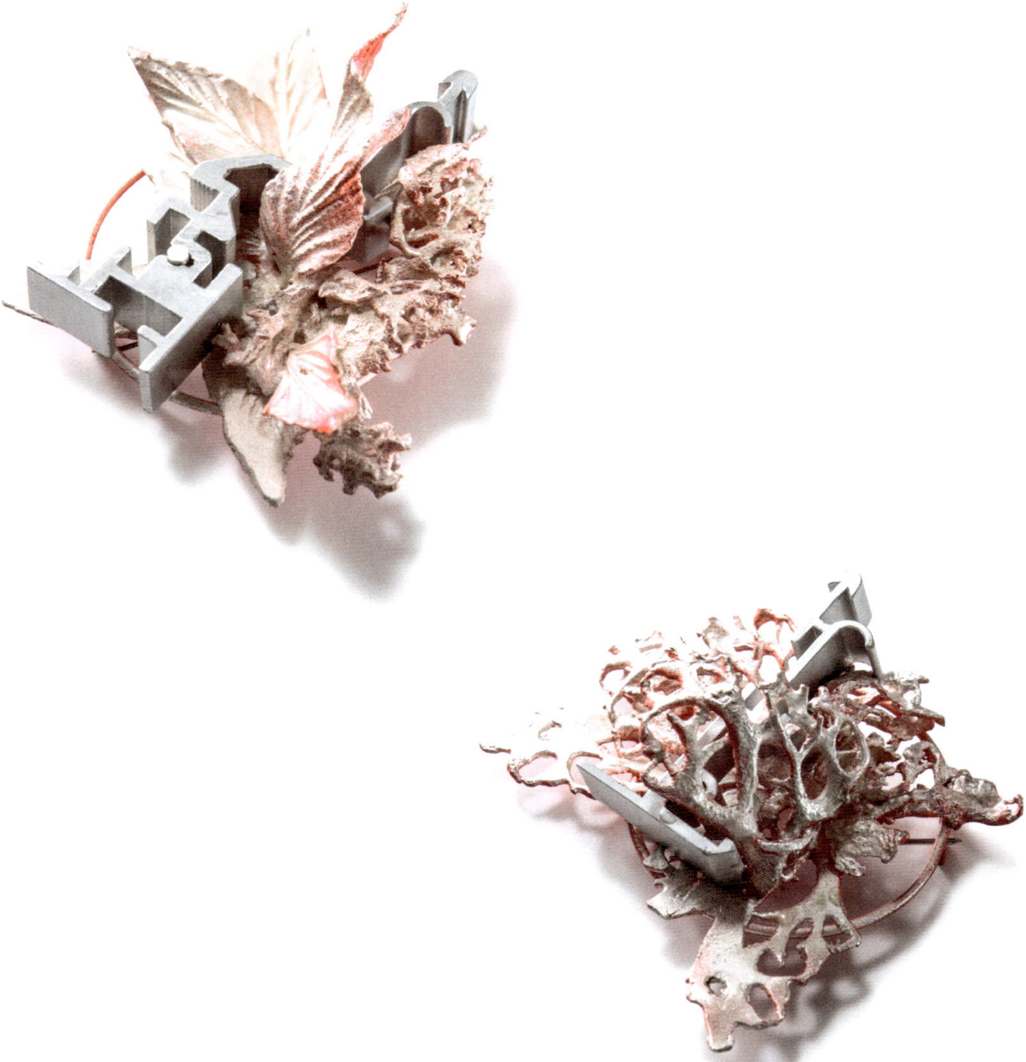

Brooches, 2013, L–R 80 × 60 × 20 mm, 70 × 65 × 25 mm, 925 silver, aluminium, acrylic lacquer

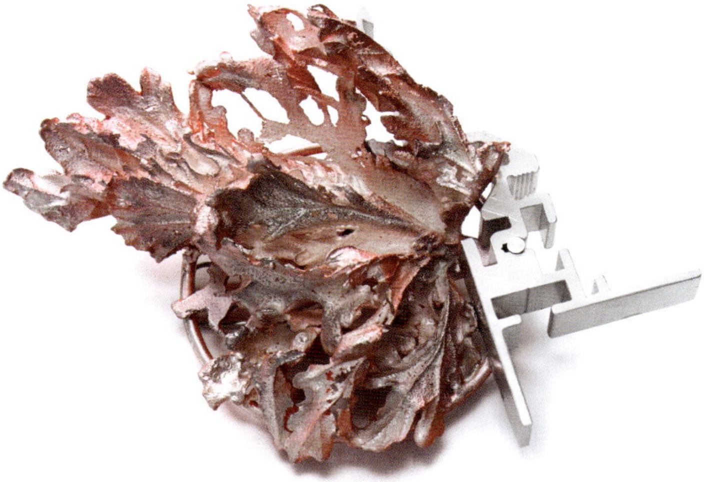

Brooch, 2013, 100 × 75 × 30 mm, 925 silver, aluminium, acrylic lacquer

Light as a Cloud,
Deep as Light and Shade

GABRIELLA ZAHARIAS-DOFF

Forget the way you used to look at the world when you go for a walk with Mari Ishikawa. She will lead you to focus your eyes like a camera travelling through a tunnel, and you will discover a microcosm where nature takes on a new dimension.

Branches of a tree against the sky. Light and shade. How many layers to reach the core? Can you ever arrive? A photograph of rocks, shaped by different shades of grey. Its reflection a hint on the nearly black, oily surface of water. Only at a second glance do we discover the green of the grass and of the leaves of trees, a different colour within this grey world. Photos of nature taken in the moonlight, showing unsuspected images of our familiar world. Images that we have never seen before. Are they illusion or reality? Taken with a long exposure, the photos allow the aspect of time to flow into the picture. Not only nature itself, but also fifteen to thirty minutes of its existence are captured in a single image. Time for meditation and reflection in our fast-moving world. And an image that will help us remember.

'Landscape is the totality of everything encompassing us. Depending on how it is framed, things of all different kinds come into view,' says Mari Ishikawa in her lecture on *Parallel Worlds*.

Humans try to rule nature, to change it according to their needs, to exploit it for their benefit. The interest of the artist focuses on different cycles of dynamic between nature and the man-made world. Wherever humans destroy nature in order to create a sterile world made of stone, plants disappear only for a short period of time, to be the first to regrow once this world starts to fall apart. Civilisations such as the Maya created cities devoid of trees and plants, with buildings as high as they could raise them in order to come closer to the sky and to their gods. But soon after this civilisation collapsed, the jungle took over and covered their cities so completely that they disappeared almost without trace. Human intervention is only temporary. Nature is waiting patiently for its time to come back and recapture what was taken away from her. Even though plants look fragile and delicate, they are strong enough to be first to re-establish this natural balance.

The brushwood we gather – stack it together,
it makes a hut; pull it apart, a field once more.[1]

This is the message of a traditional Japanese poem. On one of her journeys, Mari Ishikawa visited an old garden with ruined buildings. As the walls gradually fell down and crumbled to dust, plants started to grow over the ruins and recapture the space that originally belonged to them. This silent revolution inspired her to create her series of works with the theme of landscape as one aspect of her *Parallel Worlds*, exploring the relationship between landscape and architecture.

Delicate, curling leaves and flowers embrace the straight, stiff structures of man-made objects in her *Landscape* jewellery. Instinct stronger than reason. Clouds light as air, and a common thread of life interweaving them all. Walls defeated by the soft and uncompromising power of nature.

Of all the things she sees in nature, plants are the most fascinating. The cycle of death and rebirth is wonderfully represented through plants: from the black darkness of earth grows a small plant, the first growth and the bud of the flower often red, then it turns green, flowers, bears fruit and seeds, then dies in order to be reborn with the new season. Plants are symbols of constant and the inextinguishable renewal of life. The seed bears the memory of the parent and repeats its basic form, and yet it is a unique, individual living being with his own history, and this history is in turn passed on to the seed it produces.

In her jewellery, Mari Ishikawa uses the delicate details of the plant world, the forms of branches, leaves, flowers and moss. Yet her main focus is not on detail but on the atmosphere created by the whole. Beauty is in the atmosphere and not in the object itself. This atmosphere is created by zones of light and shade, like the filtered light coming through the *shōji* of traditional Japanese houses clad with white Japanese paper, like in the house of her own grandmother. Shade provides protection whereas in bright light we are helplessly exposed. All colours look different in shade from how they do in the light: they are calmer, quieter, deeper, more subtle. In the words of Japanese writer Jun'ichirō Tanizaki:

Whenever I see the alcove of a tastefully built Japanese room, I marvel at our comprehension of the secrets of shadows, our sensitive use of shadow and light. For the beauty of the alcove is not the work of some clever device. An empty space is marked off with plain wood and plain walls, so that the light drawn into it forms dim shadows within emptiness. There is nothing more. And yet, when we gaze into the darkness that gathers behind the crossbeam, around the flower vase, beneath the shelves, though we know perfectly well it is mere shadow, we are overcome with the feeling that in this small corner of the atmosphere there reigns complete and utter silence, that here in the darkness immutable tranquillity holds sway.[2]

Plants are material, whereas shade is immaterial. Material things are constant in their substance and bear colour. Red is the colour of life and growth, and Mari uses red not only as the thread of life through her garden but also for her objects of 'memory', her secret red, on the back of the object. You need to turn the object around, in order to see behind the visible, the surface, in a material and palpable way. No matter from what colour or what object shade is cast, it is always grey. As shade is immaterial, it constantly changes its shape, depth and intensity from darker to lighter greys. The interaction between material and immaterial and of world creates constantly changing atmospheres in parallel worlds.

Mari Ishikawa often takes her motifs from her own photographic works, where she captures the atmosphere of a time span in which she opens her lens to let in the moonlight and the colours and shades of trees, flowing water, rocks and moss, all reduced to the basic Japanese colours of different shades of grey, deep red, blue and green. Her close-up studies of unusual plants provide textures which recreate the effect of light and shade in her jewellery. Looking at her work, we can recognise parallel worlds of nature, architecture, plants, clouds, light, shade and colour – images of incredible depth, atmosphere and magic. The story, the secret behind them and the memory are ours.

1 Jun'ichirō Tanizaki, *In Praise of Shadows*, transl. Thomas J. Harper and Edward G. Seidensticker, New Haven 1977.
2 Ibid.

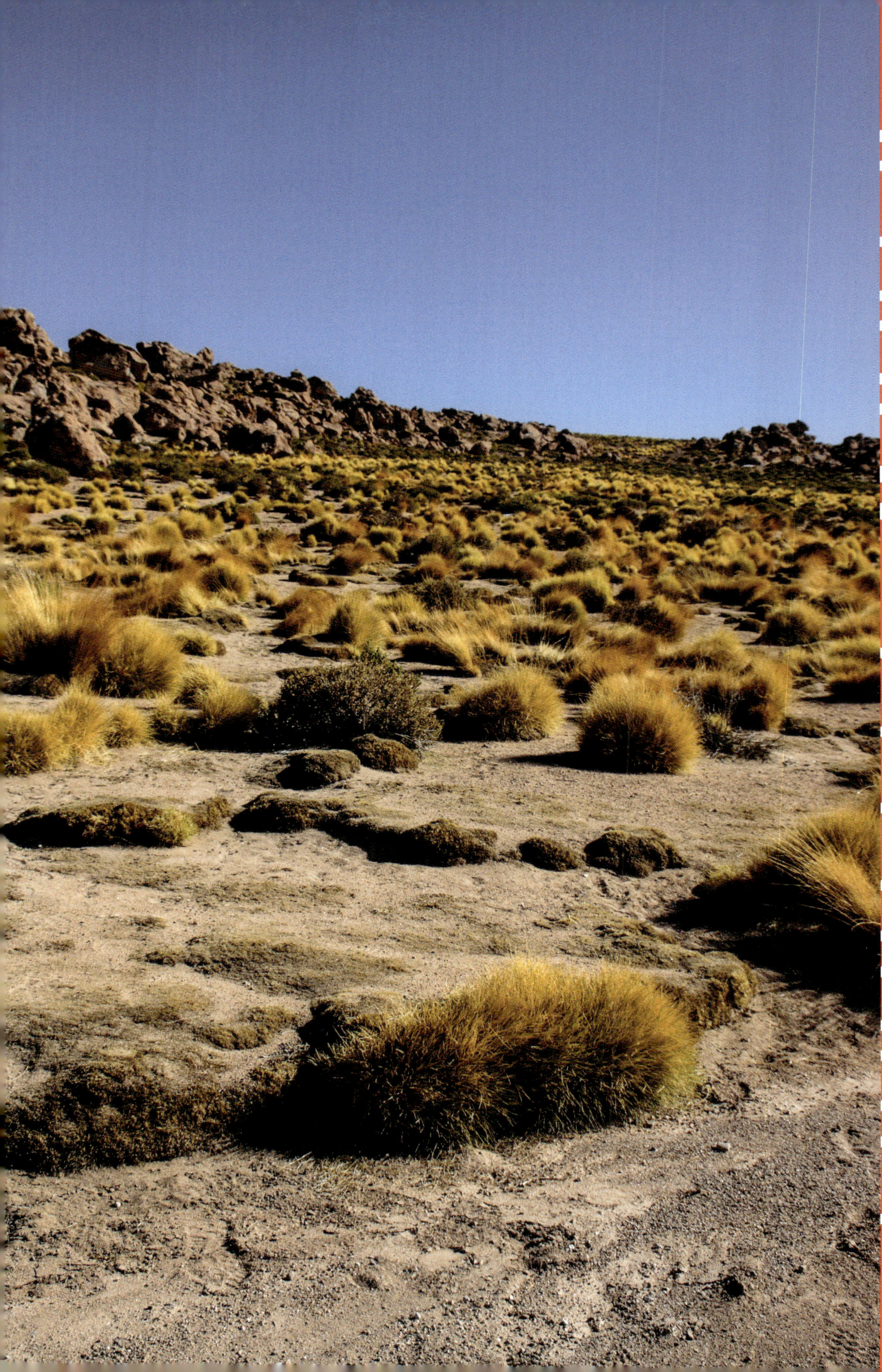

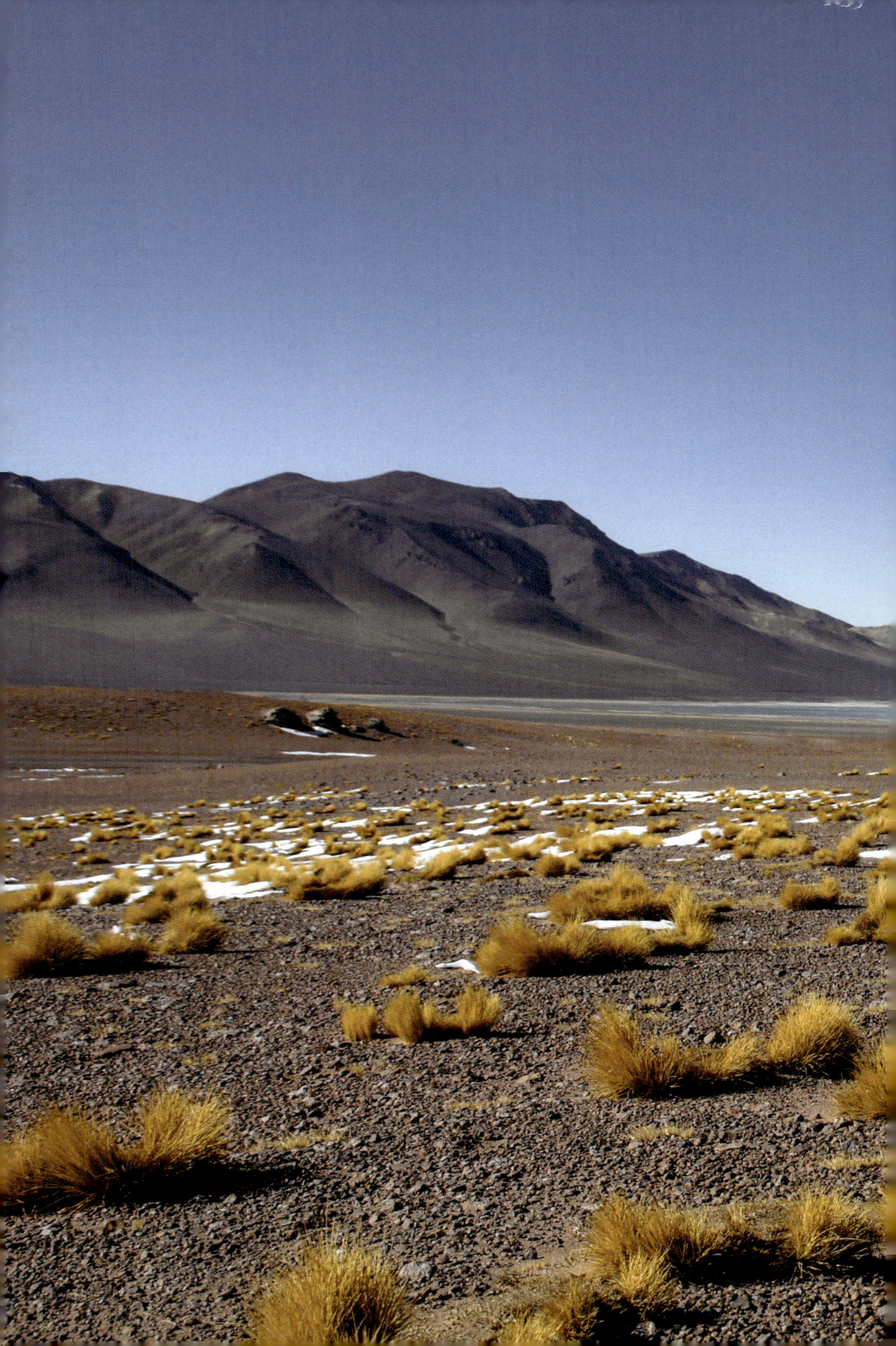

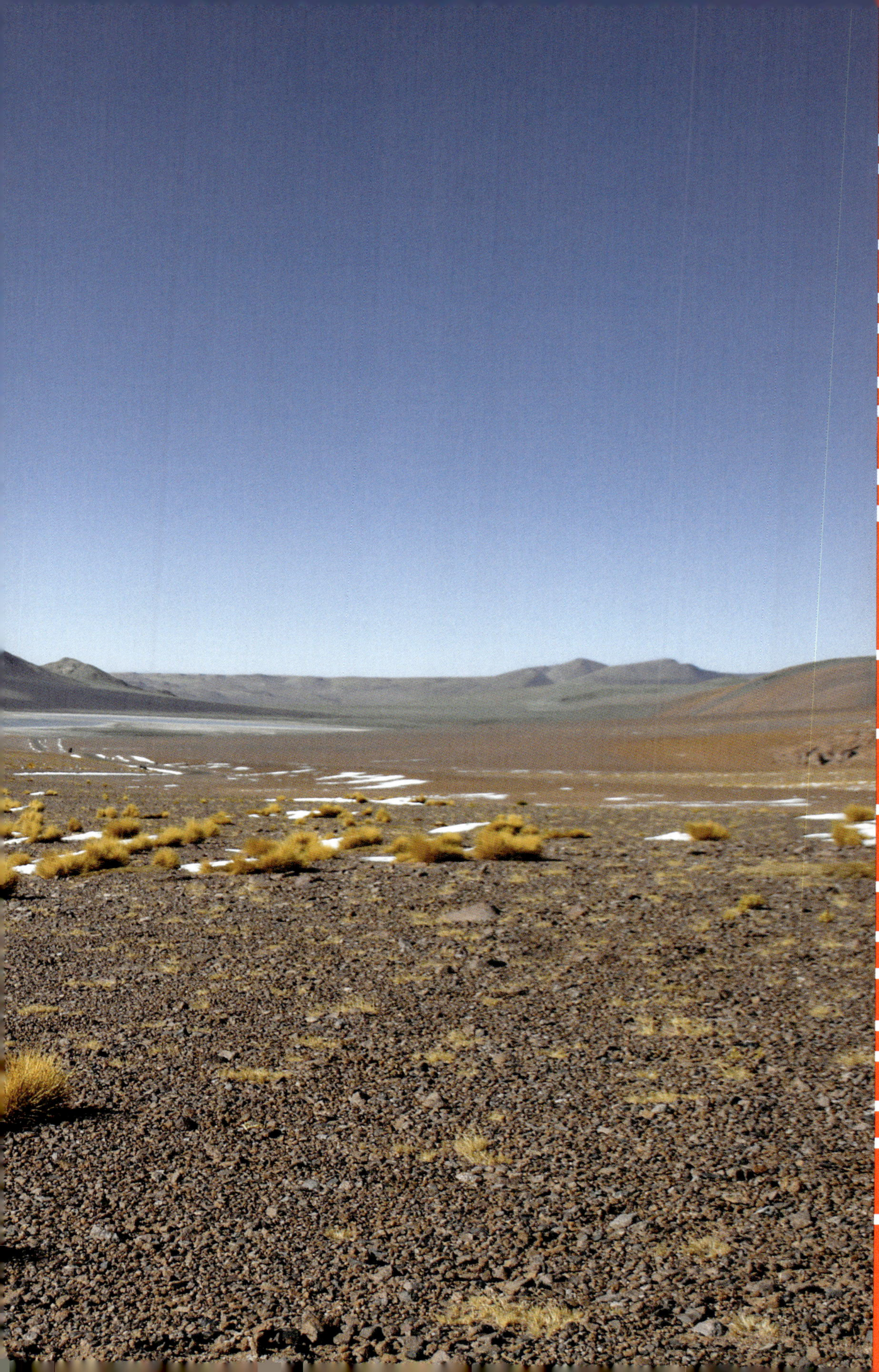

MEMO

MEMORY

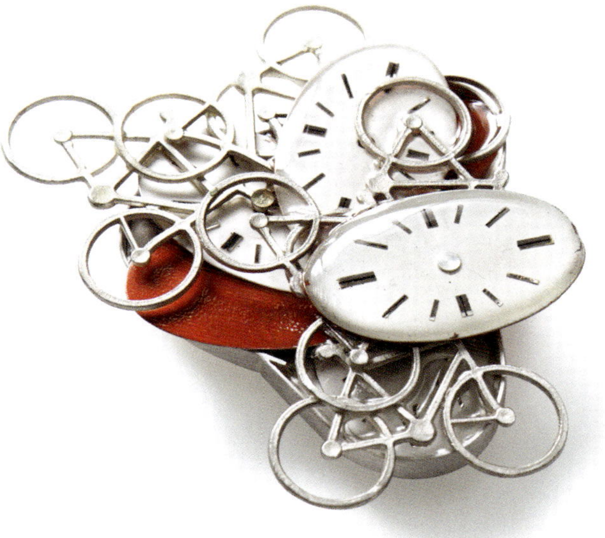

Brooch, 2014, 60 × 70 × 15 mm, 925 silver, watch parts, resin, acrylic lacquer

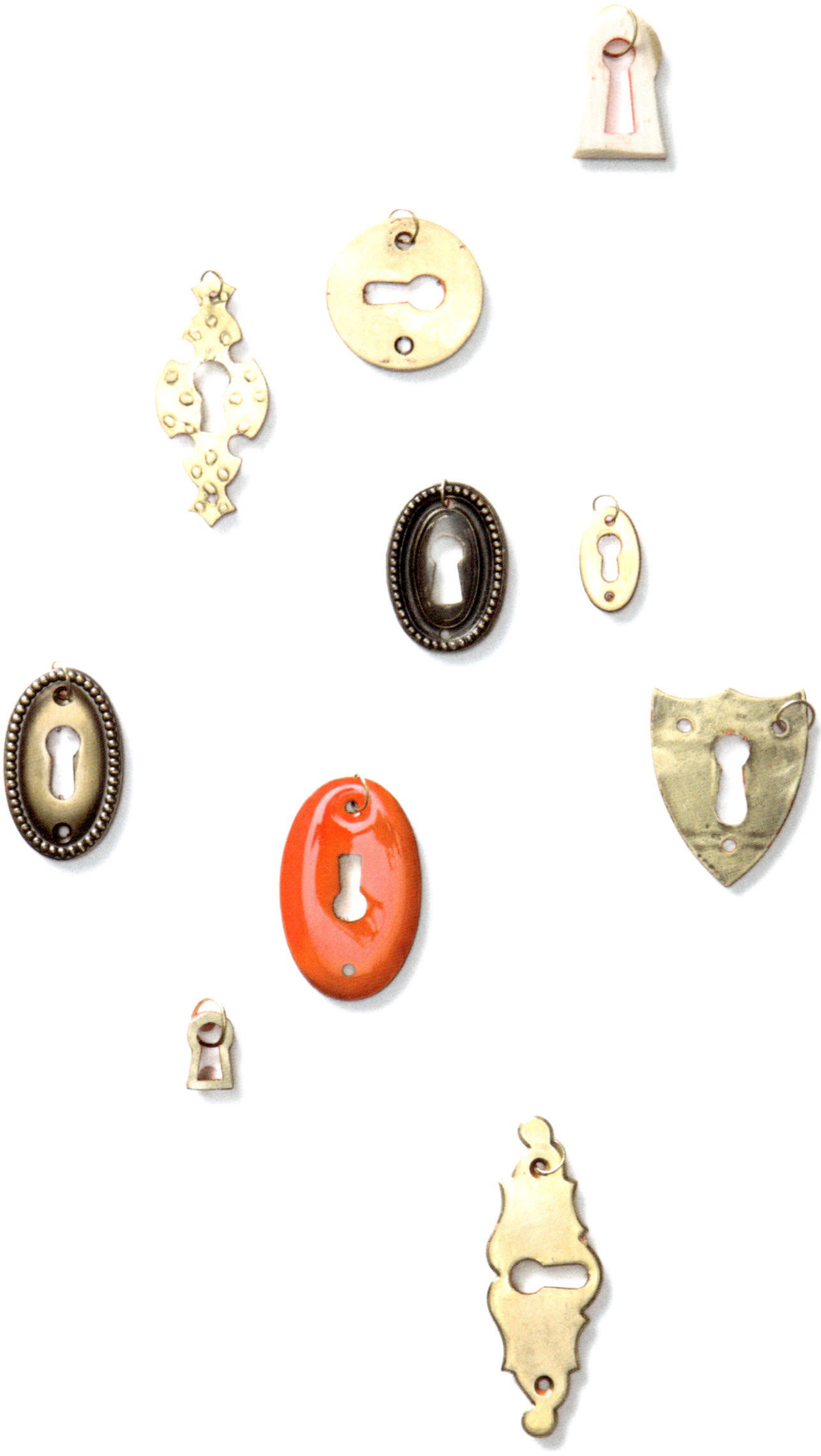

Pendants/brooches, 2013, 750 gold, keyhole plates, Japanese lacquer, resin

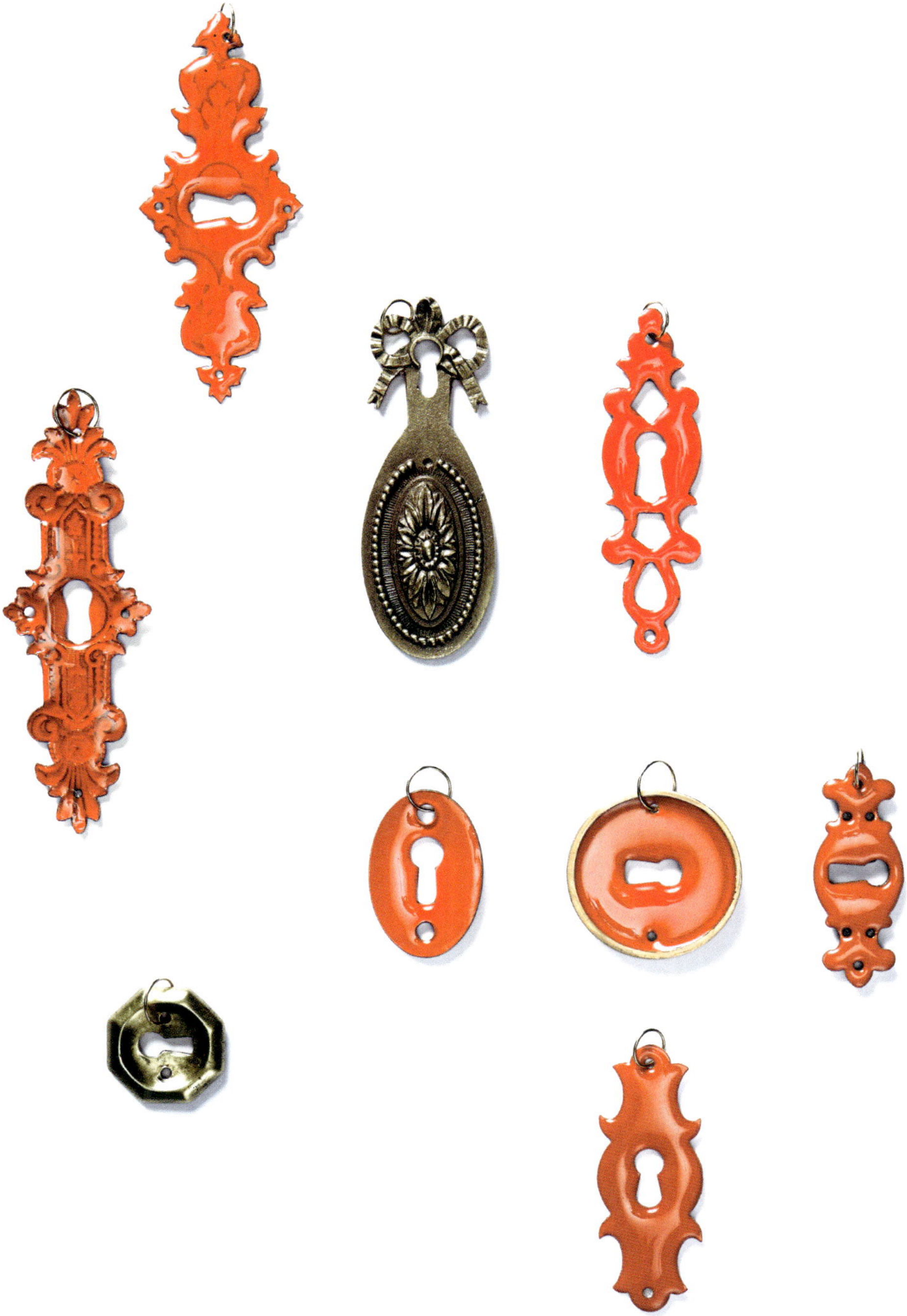

Pendants/brooches, 2015, 750 gold, keyhole plates, Japanese lacquer, resin

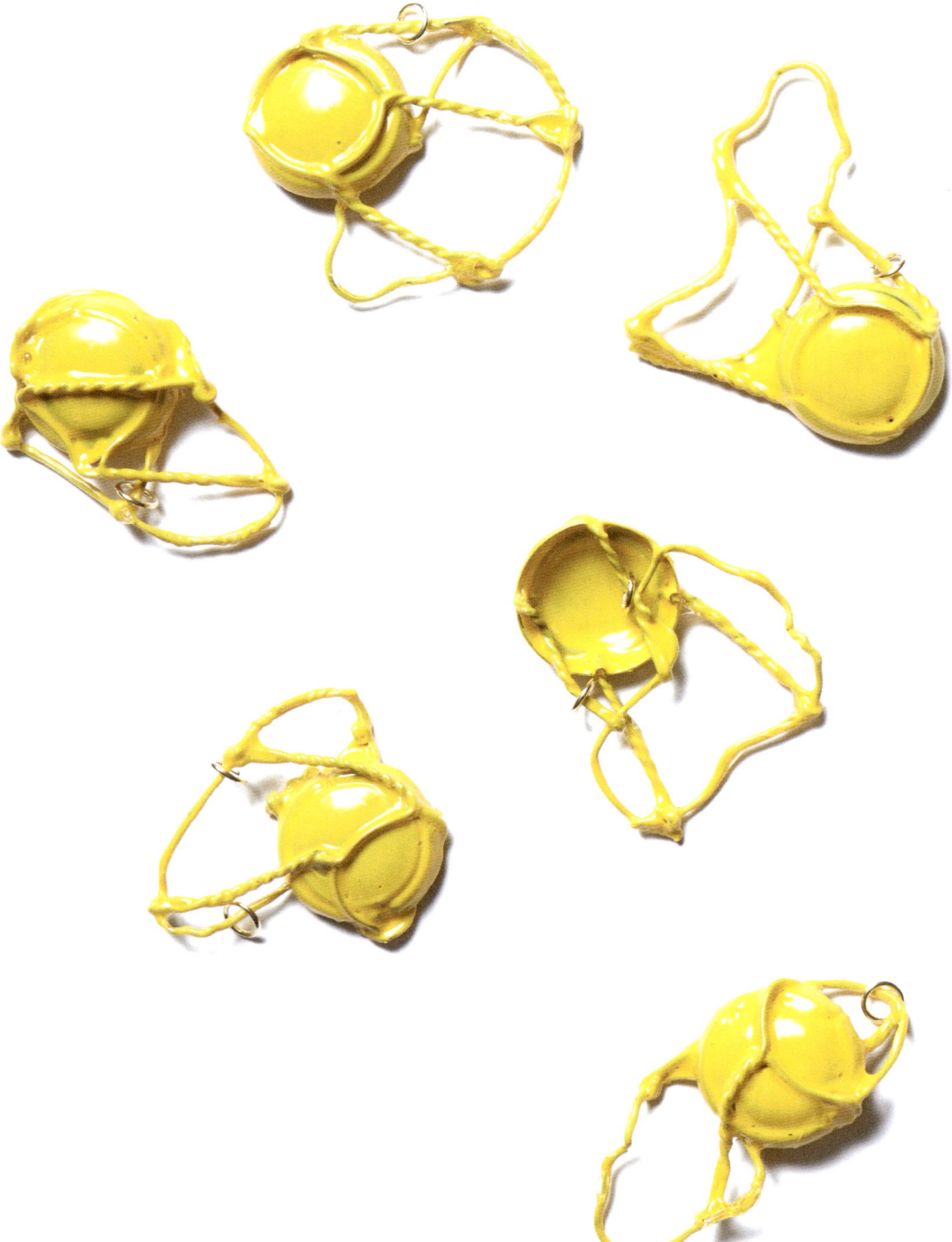

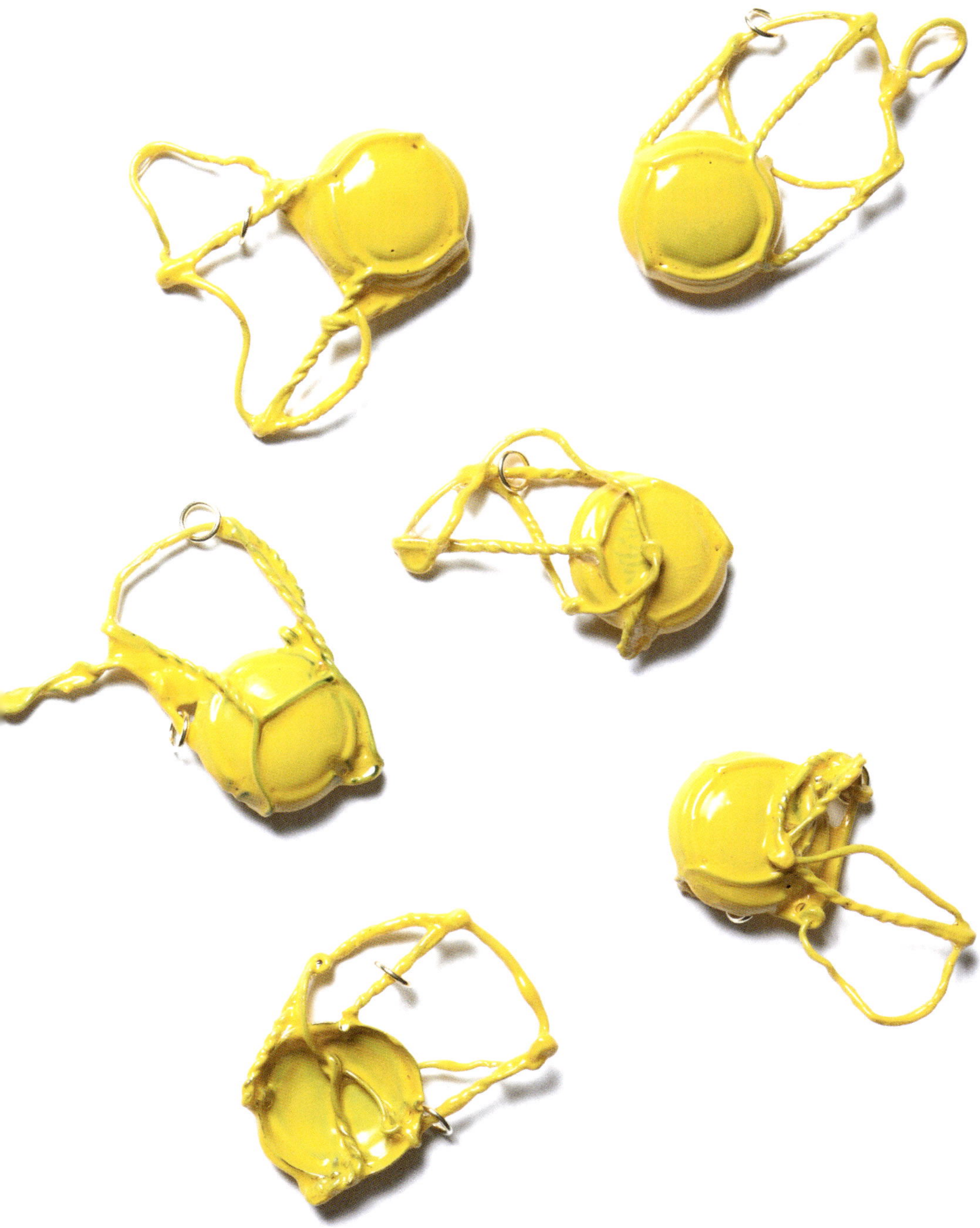

Pendants/brooches, 2015, Champagne agrafes, pigment, latex, brass, gold-plated

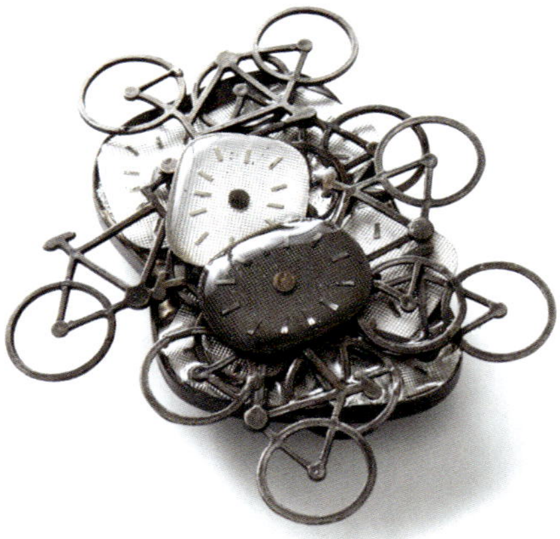

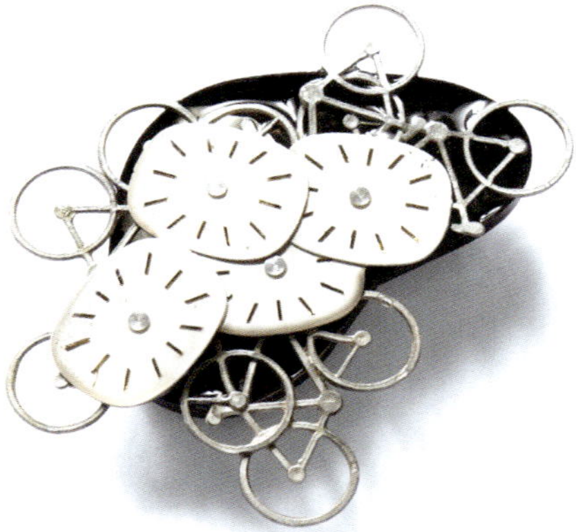

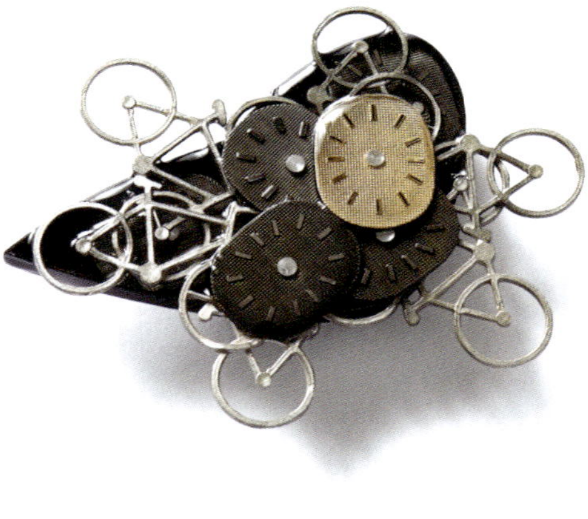

Brooches, 2014, T–B 70 × 60 × 15 mm, 70 × 70 × 15 mm, 75 × 70 × 15 mm, 925 silver, partly oxidized, watch parts, resin

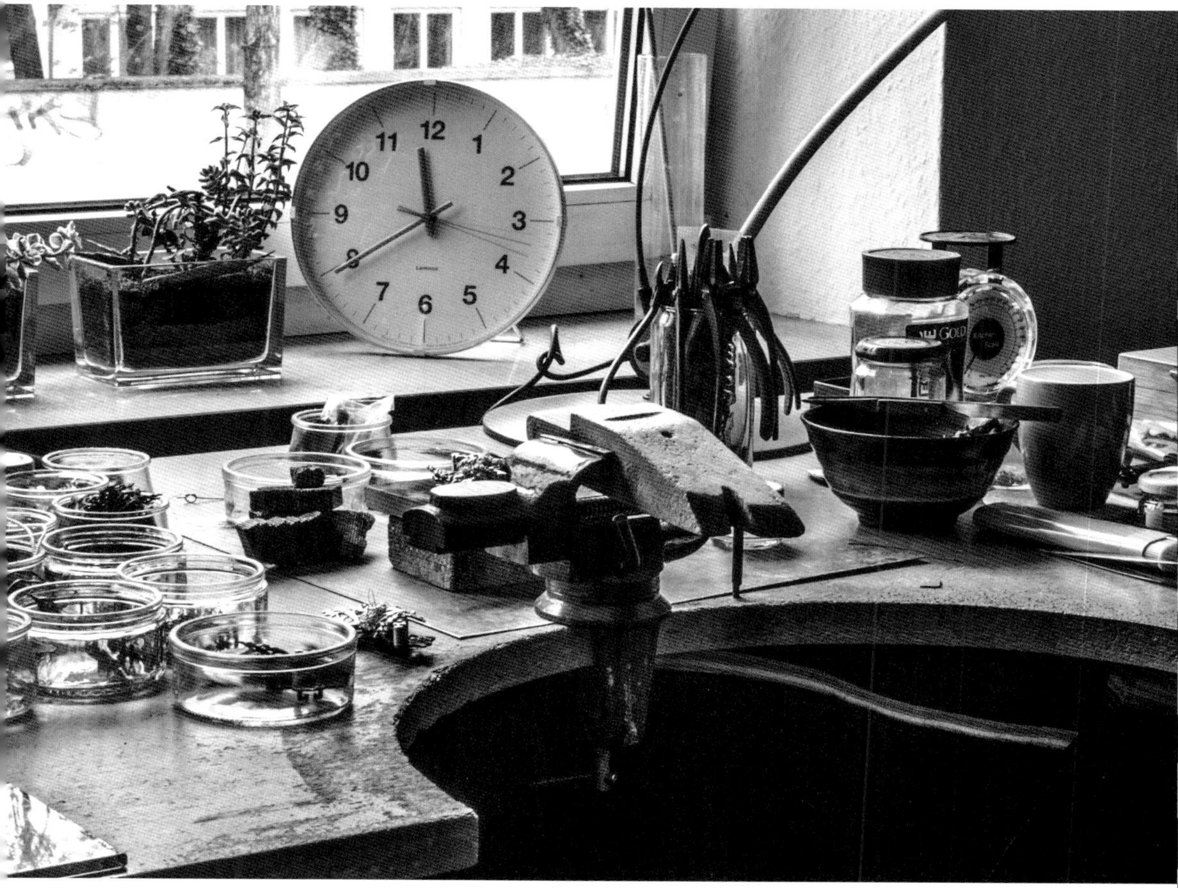

REBIRTH

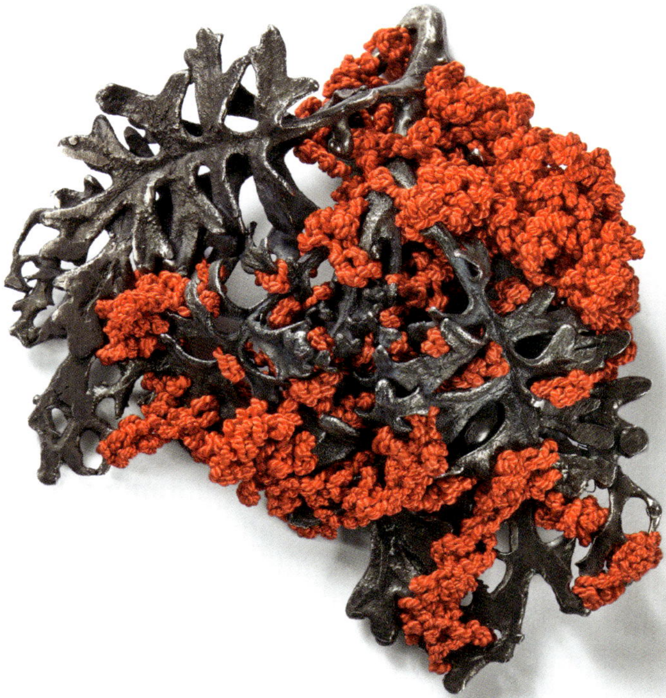

Brooch, 2015, 90 × 95 × 25 mm, 925 silver, oxidized, silk

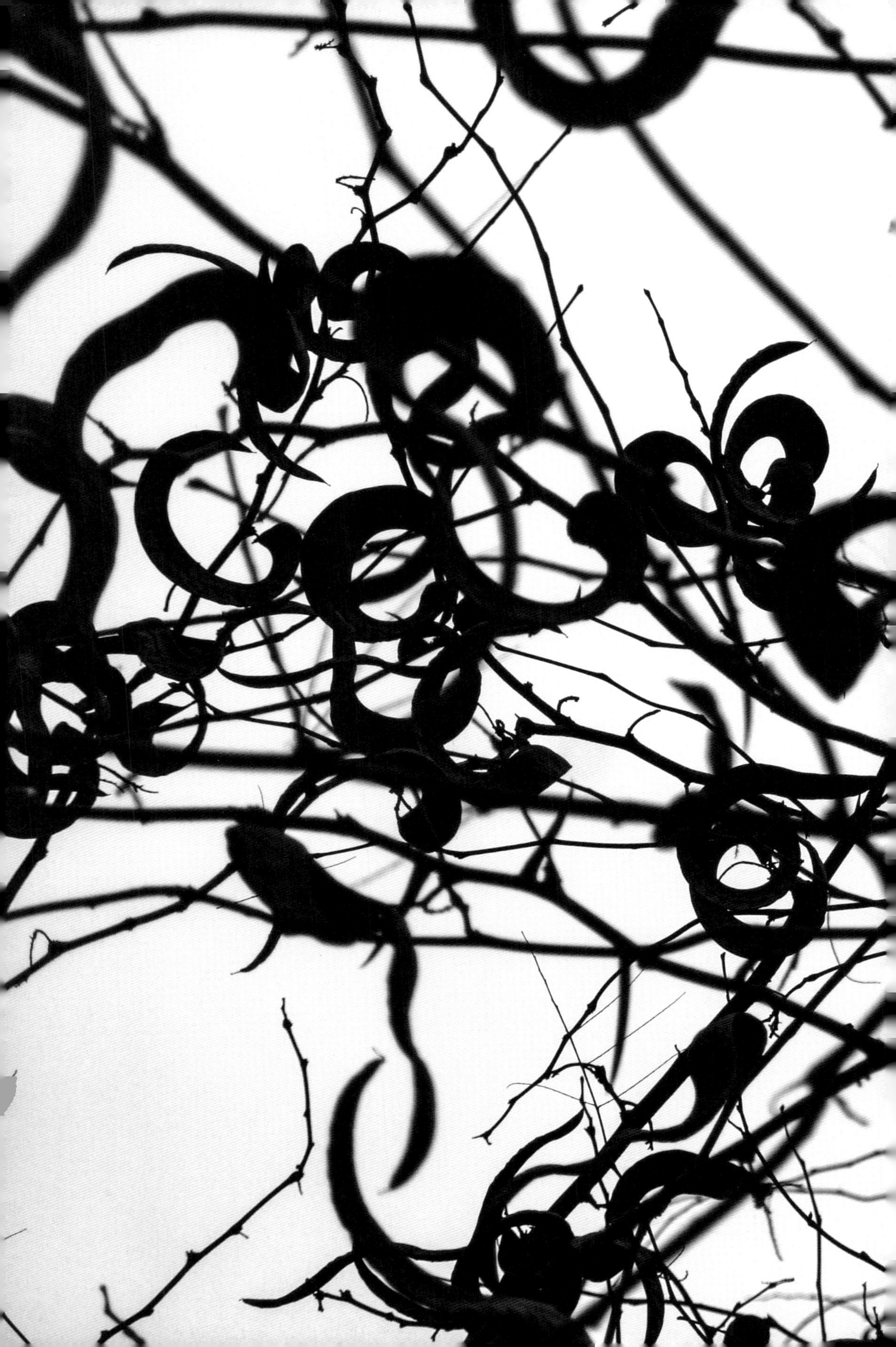

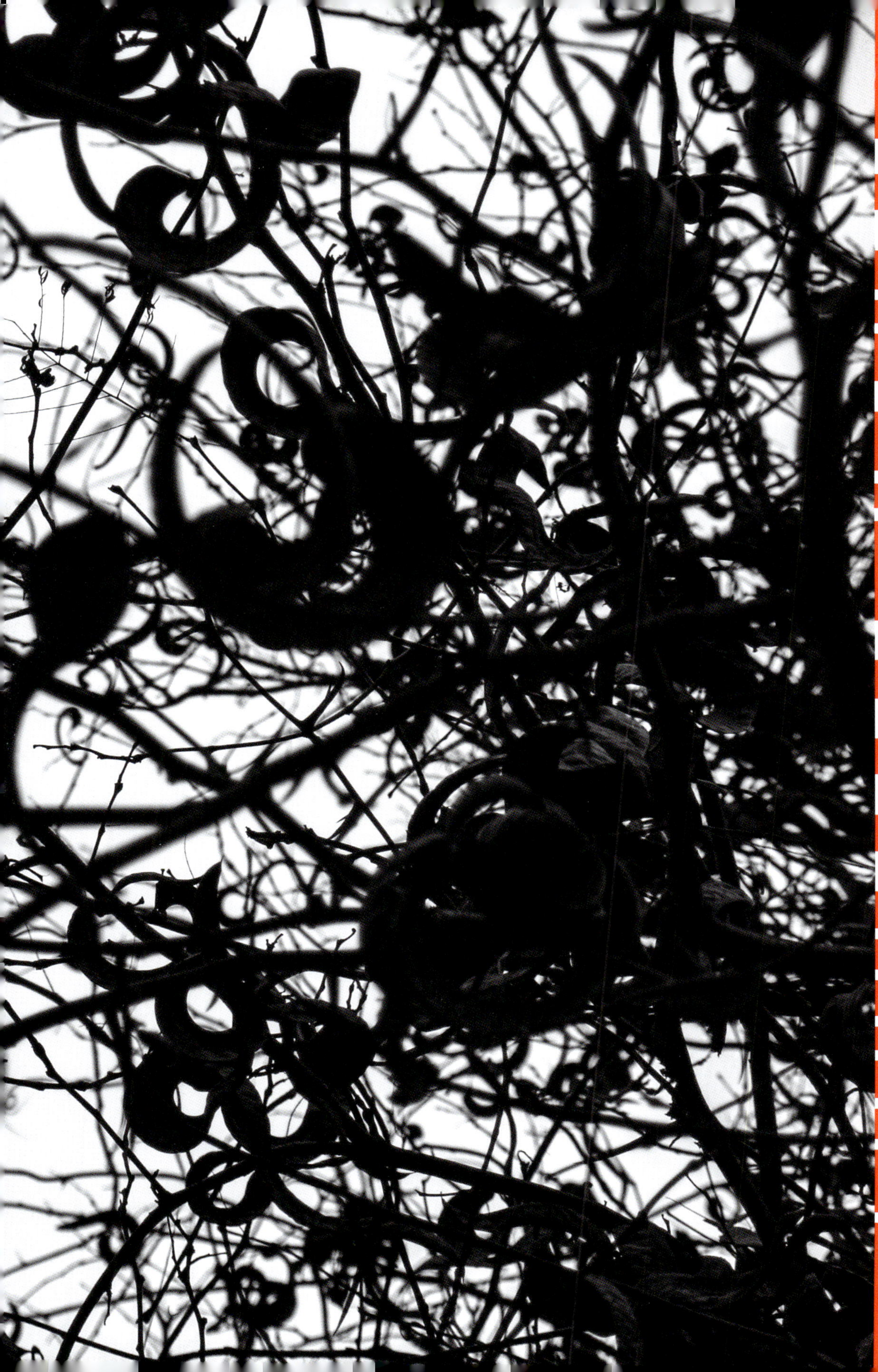

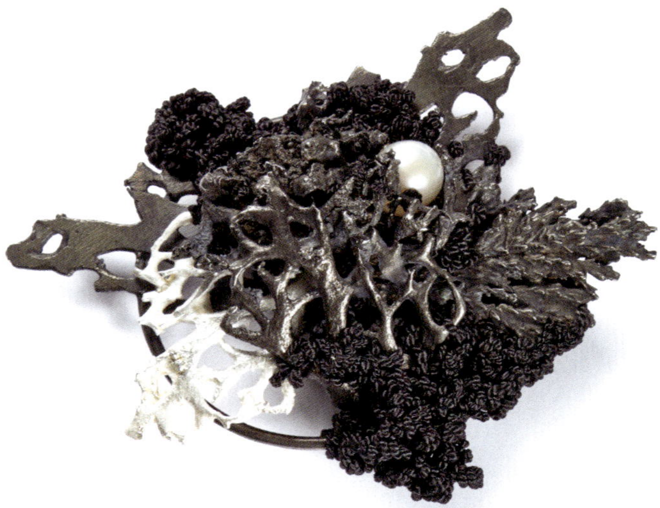

Brooch, 2015, 95 × 75 × 25 mm, 925 silver, partly oxidized, pearl, silk

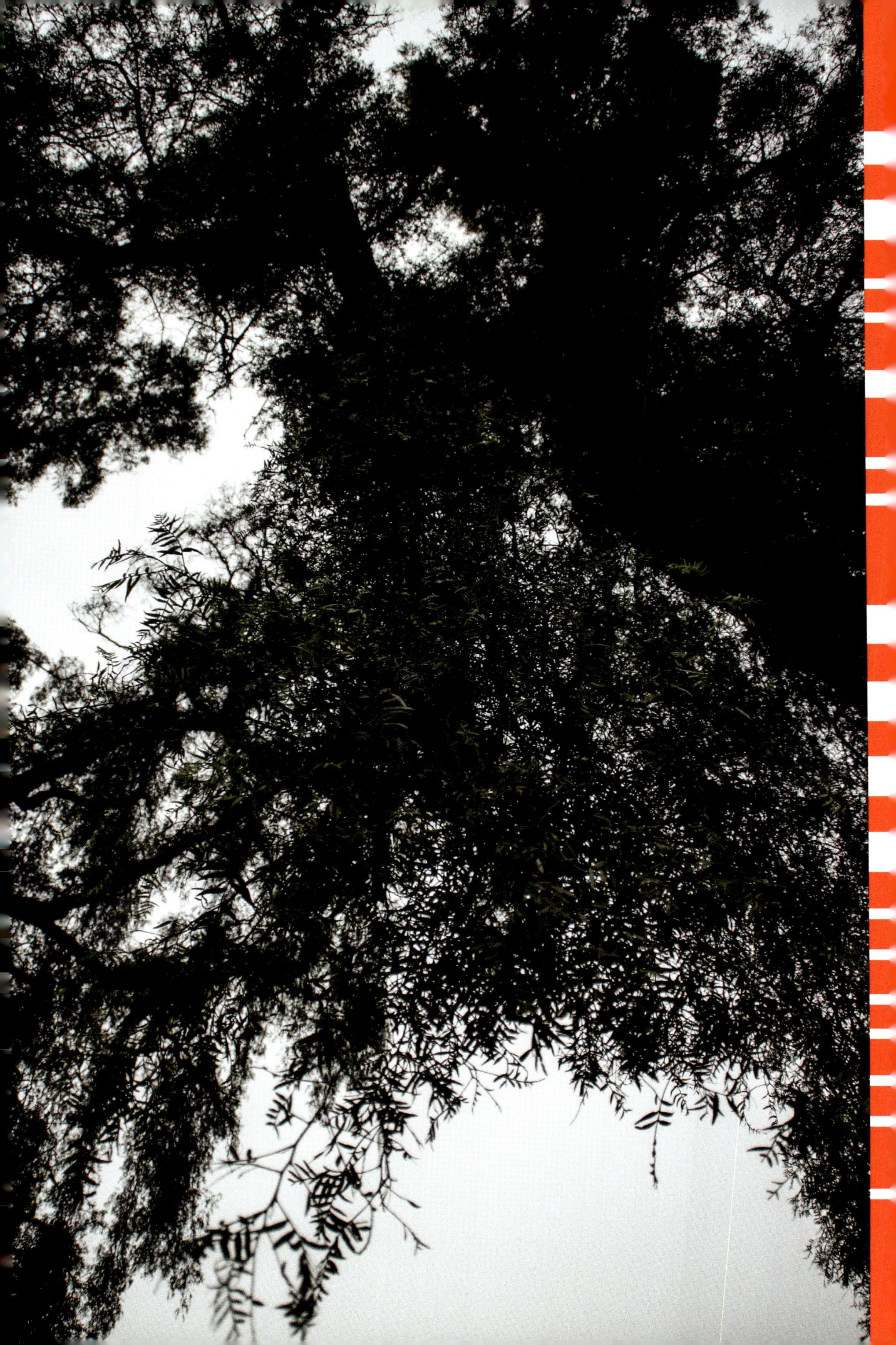

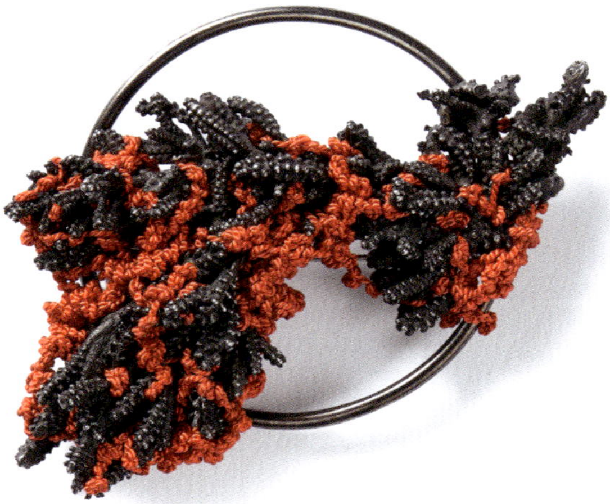

Brooch, 2015, 80 × 60 × 20 mm, 925 silver, oxidized, silk

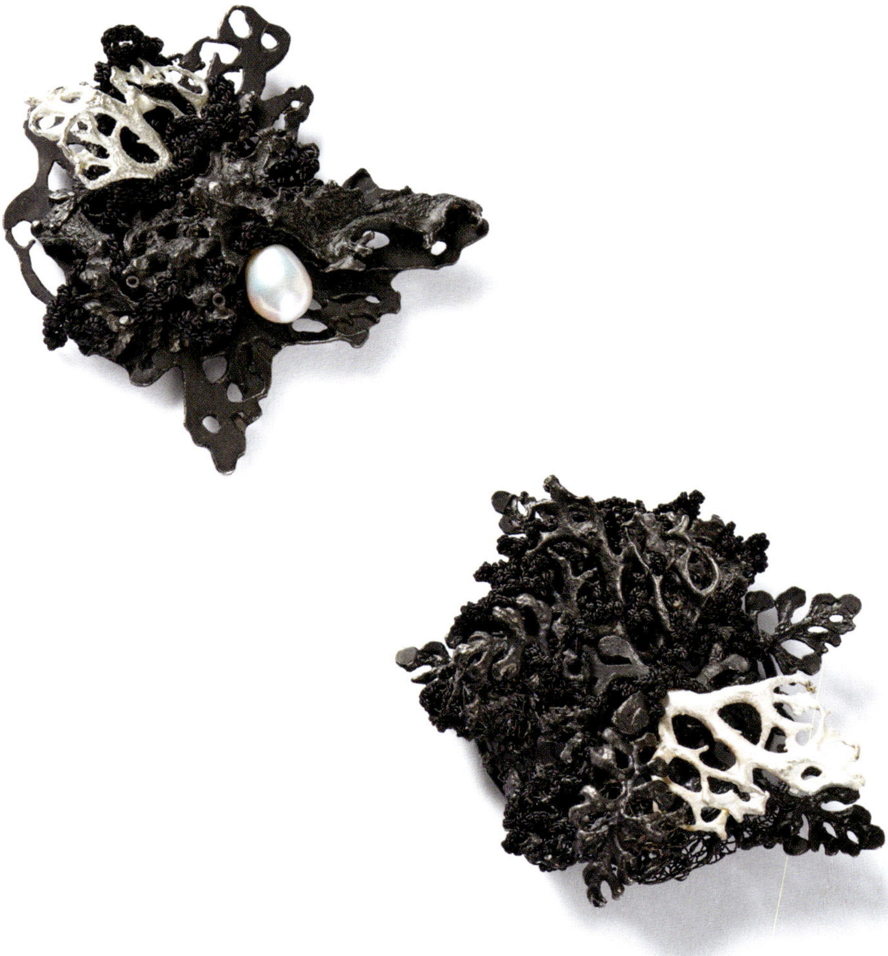

Brooches, 2015, L–R 80 × 80 × 20 mm, 925 silver, partly oxidized, pearl, silk;
90 × 85 × 25 mm, 925 silver, partly oxidized, silk

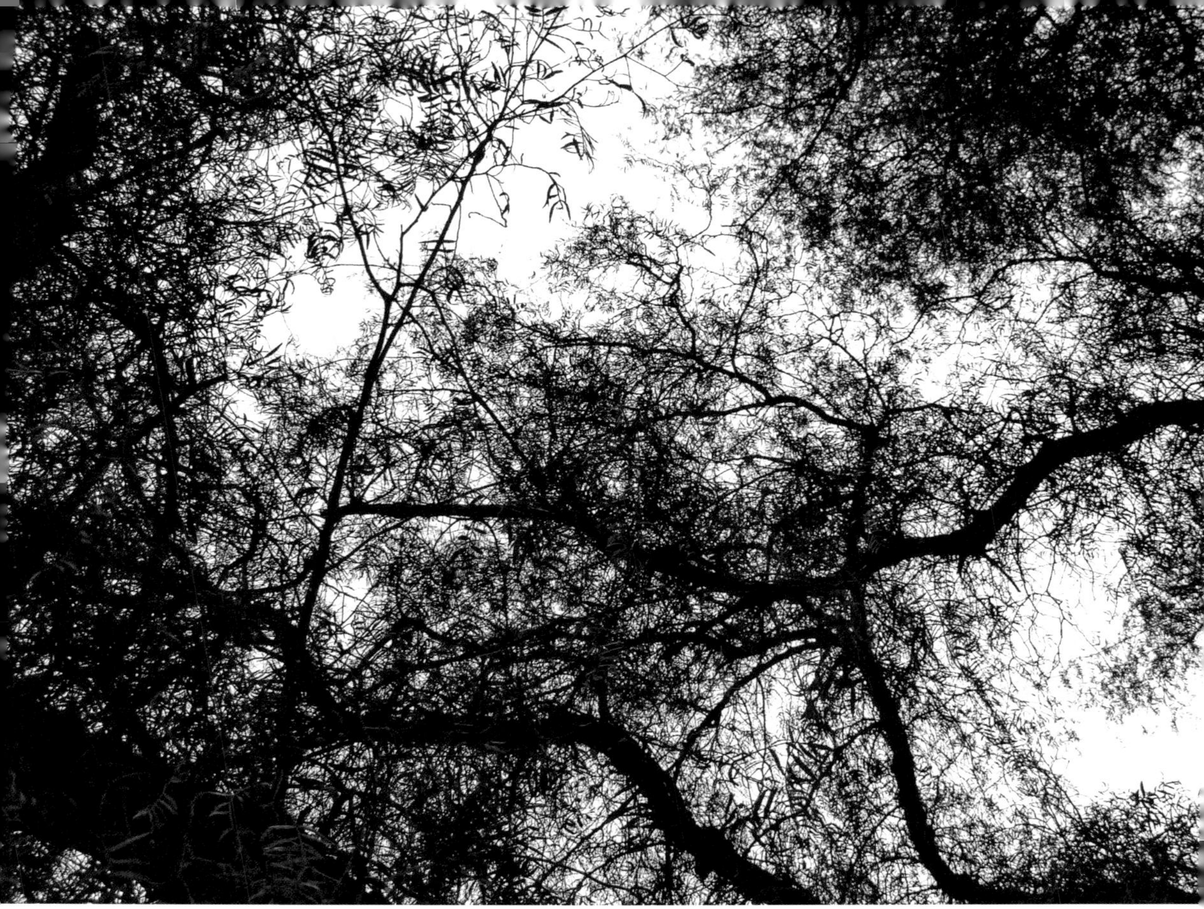

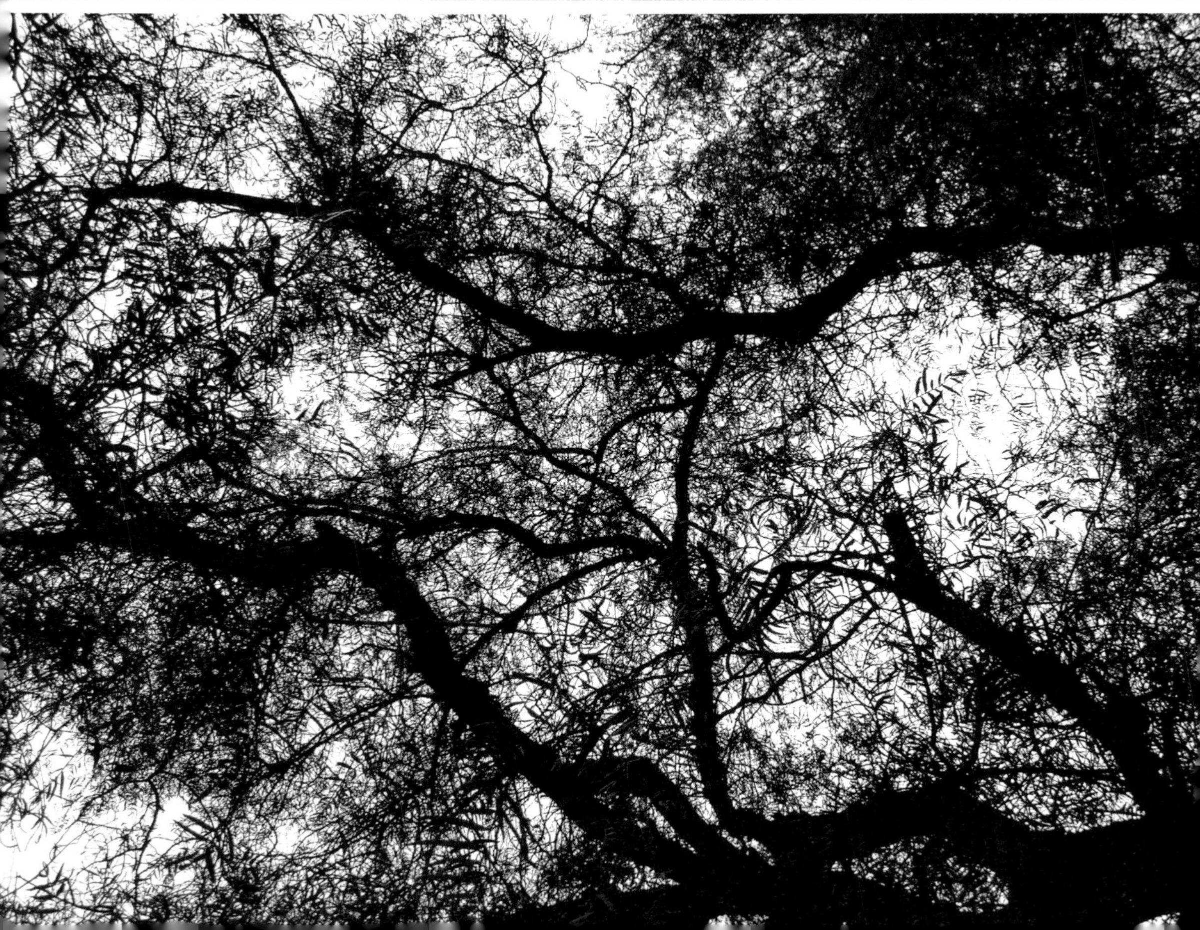

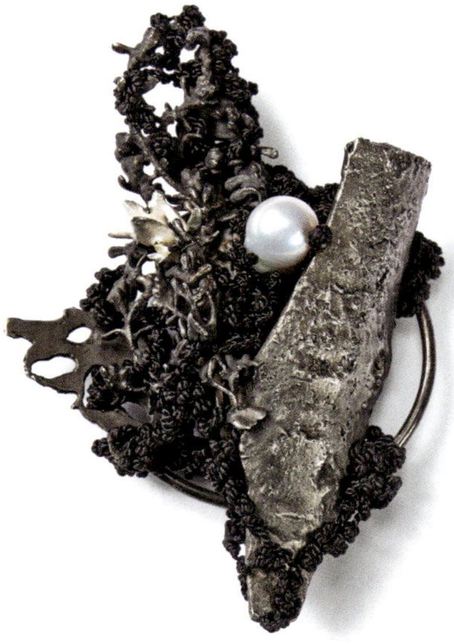

Brooch, 2015, 65 × 95 × 20 mm, 925 silver, partly oxidized, pearl, silk

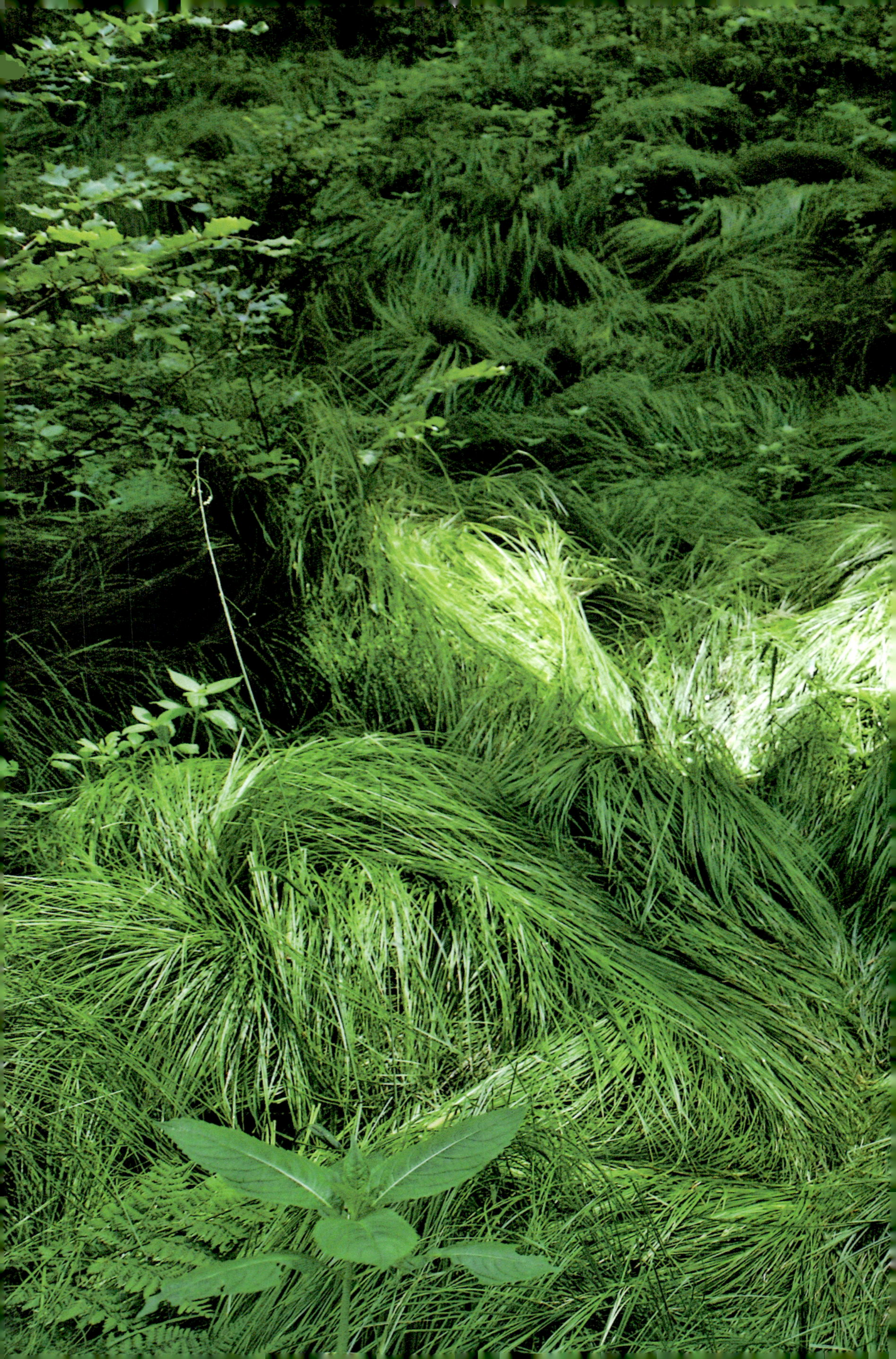

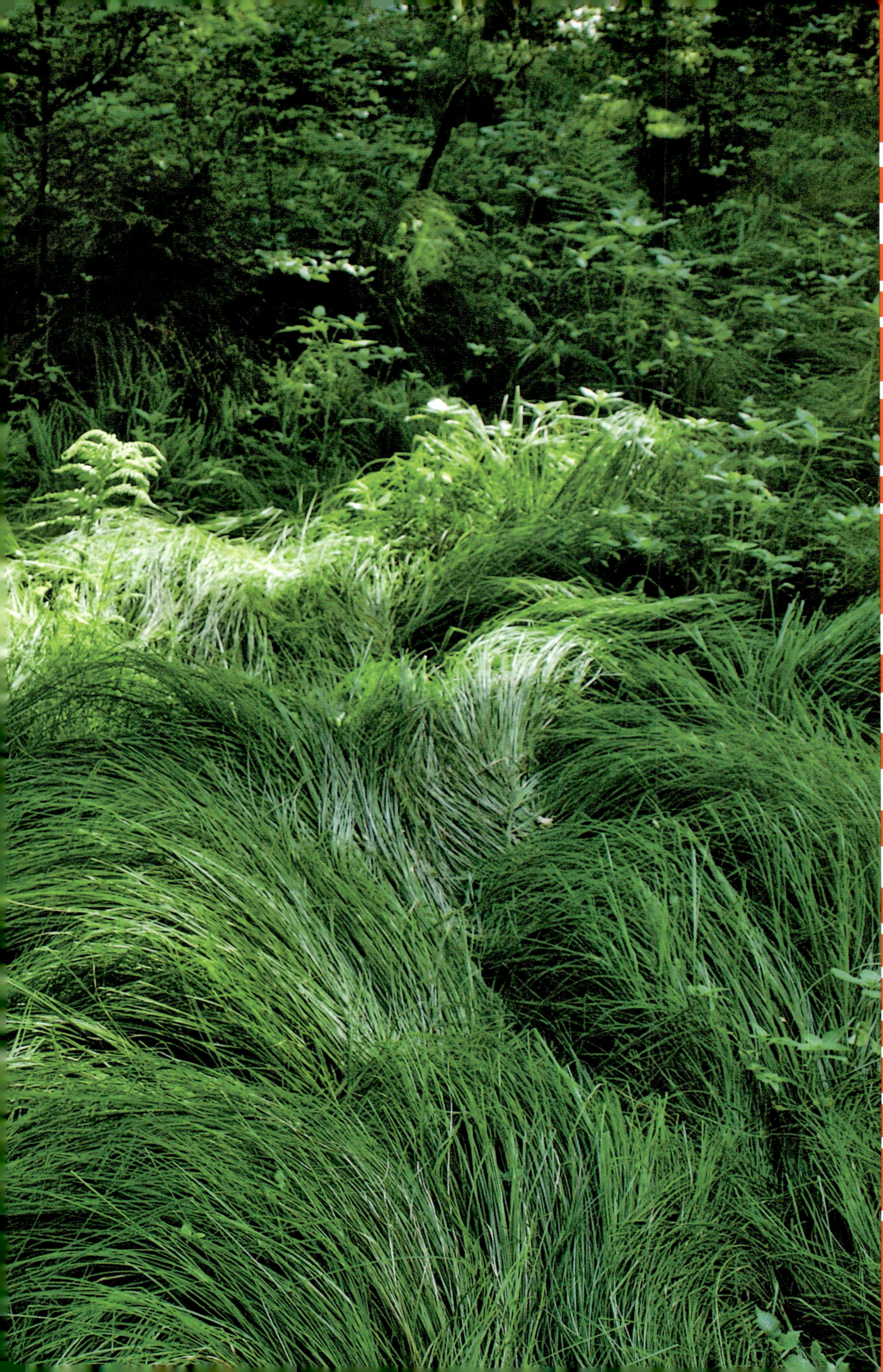

WWW.MARI-ISHIKAWA.DE

MARI ISHIKAWA

Born in Kyoto, Japan
Since 1994 has lived in Munich, Germany

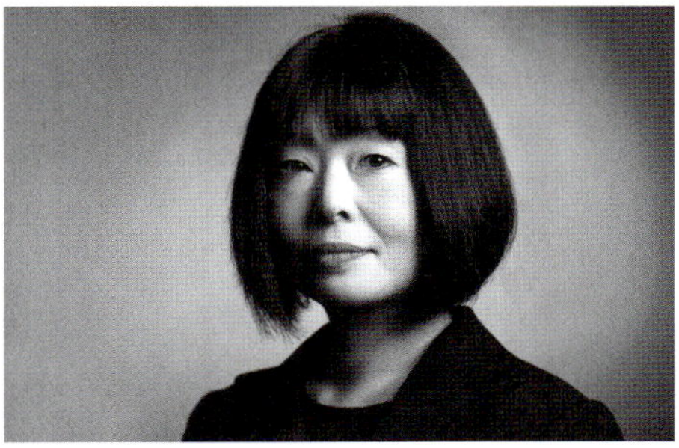

EDUCATION AND WORK EXPERIENCE

1982 – 86	Master degree of art, Nara University of Education, Japan
1989 – 94	Interior and Sign graphic designer, Tokyo, Japan
1993 – 94	Student at the Hiko Mizuno College of Jewelry, Tokyo, Japan (jewellery making)
1994 – 2000	Student at the Academy of Fine Arts, Munich, Germany (department of art jewellery)
1999 – 2000	Master student at the Academy of Fine Arts, Munich, Germany
2001	Diploma at the Academy of Fine Arts, Munich, Germany

AWARDS

2013	Inhorgenta Munich Award, Munich, Germany
	Legnica Silver Award, Legnica, Poland
2012	The Elizabeth R. Raphael Founder's Prize, 2nd Prize, Pittsburg, USA
2010	Bayerischer Staatspreis 2010, Internationale Handwerksmesse, Munich, Germany
2009	Advancement Award for Applied Arts 2009, City of Munich, Germany
2007	Tahitian Pearl Trophy, 2nd Prize
2000	Herbert Hofmann Award, *Schmuck 2000*, Internationale Handwerksmesse, Munich, Germany
	Böhmler Art Award, 1st Prize, Munich, Germany

WORK IN PUBLIC COLLECTIONS

Ville de Cagnes-sur-Mer, France
Museum für Kunst und Gewerbe Hamburg, Germany
Deutsches Goldschmiedehaus Hanau, Germany
GRASSI Museum of Applied Arts Leipzig, Germany
Die Neue Sammlung – The Design Museum, Munich, Germany
Schmuckmuseum Pforzheim, Germany
Museo degli Argenti, Florence, Italy
Hiko Mizuno Collection, Tokyo, Japan
Victoria & Albert Museum, London, Great Britain
Dallas Museum of Art, USA
MAD – The Museum of Arts and Design, New York City, USA
Helen W. Drutt Collection, Philadelphia, PA, USA

EXHIBITIONS

Since 1994 solo & group exhibitions in Germany, Austria, Belgium, the Netherlands, Luxembourg, Italy, France, Portugal, Spain, Sweden, Poland, Denmark, Great Britain, the United States, Australia, Chile, Thailand, Vietnam, China, South Korea and Japan.

CONCEPT
Mari Ishikawa

AUTHORS
Dr Monika Fahn, Managing Director of the Bayerischer Kunstgewerbeverein e.V. (BKV)
Prof. Otto Künzli
Dr Jorunn Veiteberg
Gabriela Zaharias-Doff

TRANSLATORS
Baker & Harrison, Munich (essay Monika Fahn)
Joan Clough, Castallack (essay Otto Künzli)
John Irons (essay Jorunn Veiteberg)

GRAPHIC DESIGNER
Karina Moschke, Stuttgart

COLOUR REPRODUCTIONS
Repromayer Medienproduktion, Reutlingen

PRINTED BY
Offizin Scheufele, Stuttgart

PAPER
Profibulk 150 gsm 1.1 vol.

BIBLIOGRAPHIC INFORMATION PUBLISHED BY THE DEUTSCHE NATIONALBIBLIOTHEK
The Deutsche Nationalbibliothek lists this publication in the Deutsche Nationalbibliografie; detailed bibliographic data are available on the Internet at www.dnb.d-nb.de.

ISBN 978-3-89790-462-0

Published in 2016

COVER ILLUSTRATION
Mari Ishikawa
REBIRTH: 2015, Chile

PHOTO CREDITS
Photographs: Mari Ishikawa
Jewellery:
Dirk Eisel (pp. 17, 19, 21–23, 37, 47, 72, 74, 81–83, 88, 89, 91–103, 107–115, 123–128, 131, 134, 136, 137, 139)
Frank Vetter (pp. 16, 29, 32, 33, 35, 36, 38, 43, 44, 51–54, 59, 62, 63, 65, 66, 68–71, 73, 75, 84, 85)
Portrait: Christoph Mittermüller

EXHIBITION ITINERARY
Bayerischer Kunstgewerbeverein e.V. Munich, Germany:
February 19 – April 02, 2016
The Gallery of Art in Legnica, Poland:
April 28 – June 05, 2016
Galerie Spektrum, Munich, Germany

This book has been produced with the generous support of:

Bayerischer Kunstgewerbeverein e.V., Munich, Germany
Danner-Stiftung, Munich, Germany
Erwin und Gisela von Steiner-Stiftung, Munich, Germany
The Gallery of Art in Legnica, Poland
Galerie Spektrum, Munich, Germany
Day & Light – Lichtplanung, Munich, Germany